613.90973
F381n

10/2009
WI

Reproductive Rights

POINT
COUNTERPOINT

Reproductive Rights

John E. Ferguson Jr.

SERIES CONSULTING EDITOR
Alan Marzilli, M.A., J.D.

CHELSEA HOUSE
PUBLISHERS
An imprint of Infobase Publishing

Chelsea House
An imprint of Infobase Publishing
132 West 31st Street
New York, NY 10001

Library of Congress Cataloging-in-Publication Data

Ferguson, John E.
 Reproductive rights / John E. Ferguson Jr.
 p. cm. — (Point/counterpoint)
 Includes bibliographical references and index.
 ISBN 978-1-60413-503-9 (hardcover)
 1. Reproductive rights—United States. I. Title. II. Series.

 HQ766.F44 2009
 613.90973—dc22

                    2009003662

Chelsea House books are available at special discounts when purchased in bulk quantities for businesses, associations, institutions, or sales promotions. Please call our Special Sales Department in New York at (212) 967-8800 or (800) 322-8755.

You can find Chelsea House on the World Wide Web at
http://www.chelseahouse.com

Series design by Keith Trego
Cover design by Takeshi Takahashi

Printed in the United States of America

Bang EJB 10 9 8 7 6 5 4 3 2 1

This book is printed on acid-free paper.

All links and Web addresses were checked and verified to be correct at the time of publication. Because of the dynamic nature of the Web, some addresses and links may have changed since publication and may no longer be valid.

Alan Marzilli, M.A., J.D.
Birmingham, Alabama

The POINT/COUNTERPOINT series offers the reader a greater understanding of some of the most controversial issues in contemporary
American society—issues such as capital punishment, immigration,
gay rights, and gun control. We have looked for the most contemporary issues and have included topics—such as the controversies
surrounding "blogging"—that we could not have imagined when the
series began.

In each volume, the author has selected an issue of particular
importance and set out some of the key arguments on both sides of the
issue. Why study both sides of the debate? Maybe you have yet to make
up your mind on an issue, and the arguments presented in the book
will help you to form an opinion. More likely, however, you will already
have an opinion on many of the issues covered by the series. There is
always the chance that you will change your opinion after reading the
arguments for the other side. But even if you are firmly committed to
an issue—for example, school prayer or animal rights—reading both
sides of the argument will help you to become a more effective advocate for your cause. By gaining an understanding of opposing arguments, you can develop answers to those arguments.

Perhaps more importantly, listening to the other side sometimes
helps you see your opponent's arguments in a more human way. For
example, Sister Helen Prejean, one of the nation's most visible opponents of capital punishment, has been deeply affected by her interac-
tions with the families of murder victims. By seeing the families' grief
and pain, she understands much better why people support the death
penalty, and she is able to carry out her advocacy with a greater sensi-
tivity to the needs and beliefs of death penalty supporters.

The books in the series include numerous features that help the
reader to gain a greater understanding of the issues. Real-life examples
illustrate the human side of the issues. Each chapter also includes
excerpts from relevant laws, court cases, and other material, which
provide a better foundation for understanding the arguments. The

volumes contain citations to relevant sources of law and information, and an appendix guides the reader through the basics of legal research, both on the Internet and in the library. Today, through free Web sites, it is easy to access legal documents, and these books might give you ideas for your own research.

Studying the issues covered by the POINT/COUNTERPOINT series is more than an academic activity. The issues described in the books affect all of us as citizens. They are the issues that today's leaders debate and tomorrow's leaders will decide. While all of the issues covered in the POINT/COUNTERPOINT series are controversial today, and will remain so for the foreseeable future, it is entirely possible that the reader might one day play a central role in resolving the debate. Today it might seem that some debates—such as capital punishment and abortion—will never be resolved.

However, our nation's history is full of debates that seemed as though they never would be resolved, and many of the issues are now well settled—at least on the surface. In the nineteenth century, abolitionists met with widespread resistance to their efforts to end slavery. Ultimately, the controversy threatened the union, leading to the Civil War between the northern and southern states. Today, while a public debate over the merits of slavery would be unthinkable, racism persists in many aspects of society.

Similarly, today nobody questions women's right to vote. Yet at the beginning of the twentieth century, suffragists fought public battles for women's voting rights, and it was not until the passage of the Nineteenth Amendment in 1920 that the legal right of women to vote was established nationwide.

What makes an issue controversial? Often, controversies arise when most people agree that there is a problem, but people disagree about the best way to solve the problem. There is little argument that poverty is a major problem in the United States, especially in inner cities and rural areas. Yet, people disagree vehemently about the best way to address the problem. To some, the answer is social programs, such as welfare, food stamps, and public housing. However, many argue that such subsidies encourage dependence on government benefits while unfairly penalizing those who work and pay taxes, and that the real solution is to require people to support themselves.

American society is in a constant state of change, and sometimes modern practices clash with what many consider to be "traditional values," which are often rooted in conservative political views or religious beliefs. Many blame high crime rates, and problems such as poverty, illiteracy, and drug use on the breakdown of the traditional family structure of a married mother and father raising their children. Since the "sexual revolution" of the 1960s and 1970s, sparked in part by the widespread availability of the birth control pill, marriage rates have declined, and the number of children born outside of marriage has increased. The sexual revolution led to controversies over birth control, sex education, and other issues, most prominently abortion. Similarly, the gay rights movement has been challenged as a threat to traditional values. While many gay men and lesbians want to have the same right to marry and raise families as heterosexuals, many politicians and others have challenged gay marriage and adoption as a threat to American society.

Sometimes, new technology raises issues that we have never faced before, and society disagrees about the best solution. Are people free to swap music online, or does this violate the copyright laws that protect songwriters and musicians' ownership of the music that they create? Should scientists use "genetic engineering" to create new crops that are resistant to disease and pests and produce more food, or is it too risky to use a laboratory to create plants that nature never intended? Modern medicine has continued to increase the average lifespan—which is now 77 years, up from under 50 years at the beginning of the twentieth century—but many people are now choosing to die in comfort rather than living with painful ailments in their later years. For doctors, this presents an ethical dilemma: should they allow their patients to die? Should they assist patients in ending their own lives painlessly?

Perhaps the most controversial issues are those that implicate a Constitutional right. The Bill of Rights—the first 10 Amendments to the U.S. Constitution—spell out some of the most fundamental rights that distinguish our democracy from other nations with fewer freedoms. However, the sparsely worded document is open to interpretation, with each side saying that the Constitution is on their side. The Bill of Rights was meant to protect individual liberties; however, the needs of some individuals clash with society's needs. Thus, the Constitution often serves as a battleground between individuals and government officials seeking to protect society in some way. The First Amendment's guarantee of "freedom of speech" leads to some very difficult questions. Some forms of expression—such as burning an American flag—lead to public outrage, but are protected by the First Amendment. Other types of expression that most people find objectionable—such as child pornography—are not protected by the Constitution. The question is not only where to draw the line, but whether drawing lines around constitutional rights threatens our liberty.

The Bill of Rights raises many other questions about individual rights and societal "good." Is a prayer before a high school football game an "establishment of religion" prohibited by the First Amendment? Does the Second Amendment's promise of "the right to bear arms" include concealed handguns? Does stopping and frisking someone standing on a known drug corner constitute "unreasonable search and seizure" in violation of the Fourth Amendment? Although the U.S. Supreme Court has the ultimate authority in interpreting the U.S. Constitution, their answers do not always satisfy the public. When a group of nine people—sometimes by a five-to-four vote—makes a decision that affects hundreds of millions of others, public outcry can be expected. For example, the Supreme Court's 1973 ruling in *Roe v. Wade* that abortion is protected by the Constitution did little to quell the debate over abortion.

Whatever the root of the controversy, the books in the Point/ Counterpoint series seek to explain to the reader the origins of the debate, the current state of the law, and the arguments on either side of the debate. Our hope in creating this series is that the reader will be better informed about the issues facing not only our politicians, but all of our nation's citizens, and become more actively involved in resolving these debates, as voters, concerned citizens, journalists, or maybe even elected officials.

This volume examines several controversies related to the level of government involvement in decisions by adults, adolescents, and parents of adolescents on issues relating to sex, pregnancy, and childbirth. The abortion issue has been at the center of many elections, with those arguing for a woman's right to control her own body pitted against those arguing for a right to life beginning at conception. Many of the same issues in the abortion debate affect other current controversies as well. For example, the development of "Plan B" emergency contraception has rekindled the debate over access to contraception. Many argue that they should not be required to support contraception through the health insurance premiums they pay, and some doctors and pharmacists are arguing for legal protection from dispensing medication they deem immoral. The election of President Barack Obama was a blow to the "abstinence-only" education movement, but many remain opposed to the idea that schools educate their sons and daughters on topics they find objectionable. *Reproductive Rights* neatly summarizes the arguments on both sides, together with an overview of some of the other issues in reproductive health, such as selection of children based on their genes.

Reproductive Rights

On December 11, 2008, baby Manuel was born at Baptist Hospital in Nashville, Tennessee. The baby's parents, Zach and Evelyn Smith, had planned for this baby for years. As graduate students at Vanderbilt University, Evelyn regularly took birth control pills to make sure she did not get pregnant while they were still in school. Once they graduated and were established in their careers, the couple decided it was time to start the family they had always wanted. After trying unsuccessfully for almost a year, they visited a doctor to see why they were having such difficulty conceiving. Several tests later, their doctor told the Smiths that Zach had a low sperm count, thus making it difficult for Evelyn to get pregnant through traditional methods. Their doctor referred them to a fertility clinic, where they began the preparation processes for in vitro fertilization. After carefully following the plan prescribed by the fertility team at the clinic, Evelyn eventually had four fertilized eggs placed in her womb. Eight and a half months later, she and Zach were holding their baby boy. Their hopes for a family may seem common to many, but in reality are amazing—not only for their ability to plan when they wanted to have a child, but also for the medical advances that allowed them to conceive when they were ready. Despite how mundane this story may seem to many today, it highlights advances that would have been unavailable to the Smith's grandparents, or even their own parents.

The scene is different a few states away. On that same December 11 morning, and every Thursday morning, a quiet residential street in Waco, Texas, plays host to participants in one of the most divisive issues in America today. There, in front of the Audre Rapoport Women's Health Center, a small knot of protesters quietly gathers. Some walk slowly back and forth holding signs with pictures of aborted fetuses and covered with scripture references. Others pace the sidewalk reading aloud from Bibles, while still others pray or chant "pro-life" slogans. All are protesting against abortion.

A security guard will occasionally strike up a conversation with the protesters and make sure that those gathered are respecting the right of access for patients. Because of violent protests, killing of doctors, and bombings in some parts of the country, all clinics that offer abortion counseling have security of some sort—usually video-checked access and armed guards. In this quiet neighborhood, however, these opposing sides seem more like patrons at a mall than the raving culture warriors shouting past one another as is often portrayed in the news.

What does baby Manuel have in common with the abortion protesters standing in front of a women's clinic? Both represent issues that confound many in America and raise some of the highest emotions and tensions. In the area of reproductive rights, many people hold strongly to their views, even leading some to exhaust their financial resources or engage in civil disobedience—or even violent acts. From the media coverage of reproductive health issues, it seems the topic of reproductive rights is limited to the shouts of protesters at abortion rallies on one end of the issue spectrum and labs creating new miracles of reproductive science at the other. As with most controversies, problems arise when defining the terms and then addressing the most polarizing elements of the controversy.

Reproductive History

Interest in controlling human reproduction is not new. Throughout history people have attempted to both avoid conception and provide health support to women before, during, and after a pregnancy. These interests historically involved health reasons, population control, cultural expectations, family dynamics, and personal fulfillment of both men and women.

In pre-industrialized societies, family size affected the success of families and communities. In nomadic societies, members of a family or clan would frequently have to pack up all of their belongings and children as they moved from place to place. Such moves were hard on the children and those who had to care for them, so controlling the number and spacing of children was seen as valuable. This value on small family sizes changed as societies moved from nomadic to more agrarian lifestyles. More children were seen as a benefit as they provided workers for the farm and protection for the family and community.[1]

Female children remained a special consideration in many cultures. Girls were often seen as less valuable in terms of physical labor, and were more expensive because of cultural requirements that young men be given a dowry such as animals or valuables when he married a daughter from the family. Many of these patriarchal cultures also valued sons because the family name was passed through sons. These preferences for male children led many families to attempt to select a child's sex through a number of often-ineffective methods during a pregnancy. When these methods did not work, daughters were sometimes killed shortly after being born.[2]

The killing of infants, or infanticide, is one of the earliest forms of controlling family size. Families were motivated by economic and social circumstances to kill unwanted babies, particularly those with birth defects or, as already described, to get rid of daughters. While modern people are repulsed by the idea of killing babies, the practice occurred throughout history. Anthropologist Laila Williamson explains, "Infanticide has been practiced on every continent and by people on every level of cultural complexity, from hunters and gatherers to high civilization, including our own ancestors. Rather than being an exception, then, it has been the rule."[3]

Methods to end a pregnancy before childbirth were also common. Evidence of abortion exists in almost every society and dates back to the earliest human records. Abortion was attempted through either mechanical/external means, or through internal/abortifacient methods. External methods included attempts to disrupt the uterus in some way so as to cause the lining to become irritated, thus causing a rejection of the fetus. Internal methods included taking potions or medicines designed to make the body reject the fetus. Despite the widespread use of these abortion methods prior to modern medicine, they were extremely painful and often dangerous for the women attempting them.[4]

Other methods attempted to avoid pregnancy altogether by disrupting the reproductive process, with widely varying success rates. Such ancient practices as pessaries, magical amulets, behavior-based rituals, condoms, potions, rhythm methods, and withdrawal have all been used throughout recorded history. In fact, there was little improvement in birth control until the 1960s with the advent of the hormone-based birth control pill.[5]

Coitus interuptus is the most common form of birth control throughout history. This involves the male withdrawing from the female and ejaculating outside the vagina. Accounts of this method are found throughout most cultures, including the early biblical story of Onan, who withdrew and ejaculated on the ground instead of impregnating his dead brother's wife, as was his duty.[6]

Other early methods of contraception include pessaries, or vaginal suppositories. Scrolls dating to 1550 B.C. indicate that women in ancient Egypt used pessaries made from a mix of crocodile dung and honey, which were inserted before sexual activity. Other techniques included using oils, waxes, vinegar, dates, onions, and other items designed to interfere with the reproductive process. The effectiveness of these methods depended on their ability to block the entrance to the cervix (as with the waxes and dung) or to make the vagina and uterus chemically inhospitable to the sperm (as with the vinegar and onions).[7]

Barrier methods were also common throughout history. Early peoples used linen or animal skin covers for the penis to avoid pregnancy. Others used sheaths that fit inside the vagina to achieve the same ends. These items were used not only to avoid pregnancy, but also to avoid sexually transmitted diseases.[8]

If none of the physical measures worked, ancient societies would fall back on magic. Amulets, talismans, and rituals were frequently used in attempts to avoid pregnancy. These could include attaching spider eggs to one's body, wearing a mule's kidney or a lion's uterus, or applying eunuch's urine to one's body. Special dances and prayers were sometimes used in attempts to control the reproductive process, whether the goal was to end a pregnancy, avoid conception altogether, or even to protect a pregnant women from health issues during childbearing.[9]

While many of these methods seem odd and even disturbing to us, methods of birth control varied little for thousands of years. While none can compare to the success rates of modern birth control methods, some practices, such as vinegar douches after sex and sponge pessaries, actually would have been somewhat effective in stopping sperm from getting into the uterus. Even magic charms may have had some effect because of the body's reaction to the psychological influences created by believing in the efficacy of the practices.[10]

Modern Situation

As history shows, there have long been attempts to control when and how women reproduce. Many people have wanted to regulate reproduction for moral, religious, economic, and social reasons. In

Legal Timeline of Reproductive Rights

1821—Connecticut passes the first state law against abortion.

1830—Other states begin to ban abortions.

1873—The Comstock Act defines birth control and information related to birth control as obscene.

1918—The Comstock Act is reinterpreted in the case of *New York v. Sanger;* doctors cannot be prohibited from providing medical information about birth control to patients.

1936—In *United States v. One Package,* a New York federal court rules that the Comstock Act cannot define birth control as obscene.

1965—In *Griswold v. Connecticut,* the Supreme Court strikes down Connecticut's restrictions on birth control, finding that married couples have a right to privacy in their marital affairs that includes birth control.

1971—Congress revises the Comstock Act and removes all mention of birth control.

1972—The Supreme Court finds in *Einstadt v. Baird* that single people also have a privacy right to birth control.

1973—The Supreme Court makes one of its most controversial rulings when, in *Roe v. Wade,* it finds that privacy rights protect a woman's right to an abortion.

1976—Notification laws are found unconstitutional in *Planned Parenthood v. Danforth,* because of the lack of exceptions for such things as medical emergencies and third-party exceptions in cases of incest or abuse.

1979—Parental notification before a minor can get an abortion is held to be constitutional as long as there is a third-party method that is also available. In ancient times, population size had a direct effect on the livelihood of the entire community. As such, the community imposed certain social controls on reproduction. For nomadic communities, it was better to have smaller families, and birth control methods

Bellotti v. Baird II, provisions that allow a judicial intervention keep the notification scheme constitutional.

1980—After Congress passes the Hyde amendment in the late 1970s to disallow the use of federal money for abortion in Medicaid programs, the Supreme Court finds in *Harris v. McRae* that the Hyde amendment is constitutionally sound, rejecting arguments that it restricts poor women's rights to abortions.

1989—In *Webster v. Reproductive Health Services,* the Supreme Court upholds a state law that restricts public health facilities from performing abortions.

1992—The Supreme Court in *Planned Parenthood v. Casey* shifts away from a trimester approach to regulating abortion, requiring that government regulation of abortion not create an "undue burden" on a woman.

2000—In *Stenberg v. Carhart*, the Supreme Court finds unconstitutional a Nebraska law that outlaws "dilation and extraction," or "partial-birth," abortions.

2003—Congress passes and President George W. Bush signs into law a federal statute outlawing abortion in the second trimester.

2005—In *Ayotte v. Planned Parenthood*, a unanimous Supreme Court finds constitutional a Nebraska law that requires parental notification 48 hours before a minor could get an abortion. The Court goes on to find that the lack of a medical-emergency exception does not invalidate the entire law, just the part related to a medical-emergency exception.

2007—In *Gonzales v. Planned Parenthood* and *Gonzales v. Carhart*, the Supreme Court upholds the federal restriction on second-trimester abortions.

were encouraged to limit family sizes. After the agricultural revolution, it became advantageous to have larger families, and birth control methods were frowned upon socially and regulated by the broader community. After the Industrial Revolution, which began in the late eighteenth century, economic reasons again encouraged smaller families, causing contraceptives to regain prominence. By this time in history, many major world religions had mores that restricted birth control.[11]

In America before the nineteenth century, abortion was an accepted and fairly common practice. It was not until 1821 that Connecticut became the first state to pass a law restricting abortion early in the pregnancy. The law was not designed to protect the pregnancy, but instead to protect the mother against some of the abortificient potions then in use that often led to poisoning of the mother. Major religious groups during this time did not oppose abortion or consider it a sin if the abortion occurred before the fetus "quickened"—the moment the fetus was thought to "be alive." By the middle part of the nineteenth century, however, many states created new laws restricting all abortions. This created an underground market for illegal "backstreet" abortions as demand remained despite the new laws.[12]

At the same time, contraception became a matter of public consumption. For most of history, contraception was a private issue. Women were often solely responsible for contraceptive practices; information was passed on from one generation to the next. By the beginning of the nineteenth century, birth control devices and medicines became increasingly commercialized. Advertisements for pills, potions, devices, and methodologies were widely advertised in newspapers around the U.S. and the world. In response, some felt that the "sex industry" was weakening America and engaging in obscenity. Laws were passed to silence these businesses.[13]

At the forefront of this charge against obscenity, and by extension the birth control industry, was Anthony Comstock. A Civil War veteran, Comstock began crusading against all forms of obscenity and indecency in the late 1860s. In 1872, Comstock went to Washington and pushed through obscenity legislation that defined birth control as obscene and illegal. Passed on March 3, 1873, the Comstock Act made it a federal crime to send birth control or information about birth control through the mail. Many states later created their own versions of the Comstock Act, though some went further, restricting more than the federal Comstock Act did. Connecticut not only made it a crime to disseminate information about birth control, but also made it illegal for people to use birth control products.[14]

Such laws effectively pushed birth control into the hands of the black market and backstreet practitioners. For many women, this meant little help or support planning pregnancies. The birth control industry stayed in business by rebranding its merchandise as "feminine hygiene products" and sold them for nonbirth control purposes.[15] Some women fell back on often-ineffective folklore medicine that was sometimes dangerous to the woman. By the turn of the twentieth century, women's advocates found such laws and restrictions on women's reproductive health intolerable.[16]

The most visible of these advocates was Margaret Sanger. A nurse, Sanger worked in poor neighborhoods and saw the effects of crowding, poverty, and limited education. This, coupled with her parents' freethinking attitudes, led Sanger to support what were at the time radical views. She published a magazine that dealt with women's issues and was charged with obscenity under various Comstock acts. This caused her to flee to Europe, where she learned about European birth control advances and centers where information and medical help was disseminated. After returning to America, she remained in legal trouble for her advocacy of birth control education and research. In 1916, she opened the first birth control clinic in the United States, and again was quickly arrested for her efforts.[17]

Sanger's arrest led to a long legal drama that culminated in the first real weakening of the Comstock laws. In 1918, appeals court judge Frederick Crane ruled in *New York v. Sanger* that the Comstock laws must be interpreted to allow doctors to give advice to patients, including advice on birth control.[18] In *United States v. One Package*, 18 years later, the Supreme Court ruled that the Comstock acts must be interpreted in ways that made their application reasonable. This meant that birth control and other medical items could not be considered obscene in and of themselves.[19]

FROM THE BENCH

Roe v. Wade, 410 U.S. 113 (1973)

Excerpt from the majority opinion (7–2) by Associate Justice Harry Blackmun:

The principal thrust of appellant's attack on the Texas statutes is that they improperly invade a right, said to be possessed by the pregnant woman, to choose to terminate her pregnancy. Appellant would discover this right in the concept of personal "liberty" embodied in the Fourteenth Amendment's Due Process Clause; or in personal, marital, familial, and sexual privacy said to be protected by the Bill of Rights or its penumbras ...; or among those rights reserved to the people by the Ninth Amendment....

The Constitution does not explicitly mention any right of privacy. In a line of decisions, however, going back perhaps as far as *Union Pacific R. Co. v. Botsford*, 141 U.S. 250, 251 (1891), the Court has recognized that a right of personal privacy, or a guarantee of certain areas or zones of privacy, does exist under the Constitution.... This right of privacy, whether it be founded in the Fourteenth Amendment's concept of personal liberty and restrictions upon state action, as we feel it is, or, as the District Court determined, in the Ninth Amendment's reservation of rights to the people, is broad enough to encompass a woman's decision whether or not to terminate her pregnancy.

We, therefore, conclude that the right of personal privacy includes the abortion decision, but that this right is not unqualified and must be considered against important state interests in regulation.

Sanger's influence led to a broader discussion in America about medical information and privacy of couples and individuals. Following the successes of the previous cases, reproductive-rights advocates pushed a test case through the courts. In 1965, the Supreme Court addressed the question of marital privacy and the right in *Griswold v. Connecticut*. Dr. Charles Lee Buxton, a Planned Parenthood doctor, and Estelle Griswold, director of a Planned Parenthood clinic, were arrested for providing birth control information and devices to married couples at a time when birth control was illegal in Connecticut. After working its

In view of all this, we do not agree that, by adopting one theory of life, Texas may override the rights of the pregnant woman that are at stake. We repeat, however, that the State does have an important and legitimate interest in preserving and protecting the health of the pregnant woman, whether she be a resident of the State or a nonresident who seeks medical consultation and treatment there, and that it has still another important and legitimate interest in protecting the potentiality of human life. These interests are separate and distinct. Each grows in substantiality as the woman approaches term and, at a point during pregnancy, each becomes "compelling."

This holding, we feel, is consistent with the relative weights of the respective interests involved, with the lessons and examples of medical and legal history, with the lenity of the common law, and with the demands of the profound problems of the present day. The decision leaves the State free to place increasing restrictions on abortion as the period of pregnancy lengthens, so long as those restrictions are tailored to the recognized state interests. The decision vindicates the right of the physician to administer medical treatment according to his professional judgment up to the points where important state interests provide compelling justifications for intervention. Up to those points, the abortion decision in all its aspects is inherently, and primarily, a medical decision, and basic responsibility for it must rest with the physician. If an individual practitioner abuses the privilege of exercising proper medical judgment, the usual remedies, judicial and intraprofessional, are available.

way to the Supreme Court, the case was decided in a 7–2 ruling that there exists a right to privacy found in the "penumbras" of several of the first 10 amendments to the Constitution. This meant that a marital zone of privacy existed and that Connecticut could not restrict couples from using birth control. Seven years later, in *Eisenstadt v. Baird*, the Supreme Court extended this same right of privacy to unmarried individuals who also wished to use birth control.[20]

The issue of abortion came to national prominence a decade after the courts decided in favor of birth control privacy. In 1973, the case of *Roe v. Wade* refocused attention on reproductive health by establishing that abortion fell under a woman's right to privacy; therefore, states could not completely restrict abortion. This began a contentious battle over the limits a state can place on abortion that continues to this day.[21]

An early attempt by states to regulate abortion after the *Roe* decision had to do with notification laws. Several states had laws that required either a minor's parents or a woman's spouse to be notified before a doctor could perform an abortion. For those who supported these restrictions, notification laws were a good way to make sure parental rights were protected or that access to abortions was limited. For opponents of such laws, notification laws were seen as interferences in a woman's right to choose. Some argued that it was illogical and even unethical to require such notifications in cases where the woman was impregnated because of incest or if some other abuse were occurring. The Supreme Court first examined this issue in *Planned Parenthood v. Danforth*. In *Danforth*, the Court struck down a Missouri law that required a woman to tell her husband before she had an abortion and required minors to get written permission from parents before the procedure could occur. The Court found that the state could not give complete control over whether a woman has an abortion to either her husband or her parent, if she were a minor. Such blanket powers violated a woman's constitutional rights.[22]

The year 1976 was the high point of constitutional protection for abortions. Since that time, various cases and laws have limited a woman's ability to have an abortion. In 1977, the Supreme Court ruled in *Maher v. Roe* that state restrictions on public funding for abortions were constitutional. Three years later, in *Harris v. McRae*, the Court made the same finding for restrictions on federal funding. In 1989, the Court upheld a Missouri law that disallowed public facilities to perform abortions unless it was medically necessary. Taken together, these laws greatly affected the legal landscape for states attempting to regulate abortions and individuals who were seeking them.[23]

In 1992, the Supreme Court took the case of *Planned Parenthood v. Casey*, in which abortion providers had sued to get the Pennsylvania Abortion Control Act declared unconstitutional. The petitioners argued that parental notification, a 24-hour waiting period, spousal notification, and various reporting requirements for abortion providers constituted a violation of a woman's right to privacy in medical matters. Writing the majority opinion for the Court, Justice Sandra Day O'Connor held that *Roe* was still the law and the right to an abortion was still protected, but she went on to explain that, "[the Court] thinks that . . . all the provisions at issue here except that relating to spousal notice are constitutional."[24]

Since 1992, specifics related to abortion have cropped up occasionally, including the question of which methods are acceptable (i.e. "partial-birth abortion") and whether the federal government can determine when abortions are not allowed.[25] The abortion debate has consumed the political process, both for those seeking elected office and those seeking to be appointed to either the executive or legislative branches of government. An abortion "litmus test" has become popular with both social conservatives and liberals—that if a person disagrees with a particular view of abortion, then they would not be considered or confirmed for certain government positions.[26]

The law has also had to respond to the way the abortion debate has played out in American society. After abortion clinics were bombed and doctors were shot in incidents across the country, laws were passed to protect access and provide safety buffers to clinics. These laws were met with concern about protecting the rights of abortion opponents to protest in front of clinics. Other abortion-related laws have had incidental effects on areas such as protecting pregnant women from domestic violence, funding for public health, and racial discrimination.[27]

Yet the question remains—if reproduction and attempts to control it have been used for centuries, why are people still arguing about these various issues? One answer lies in the advanced technology now available to those seeking to control reproduction.

Technology

In industrialized societies, technological advances have benefited women and families in many ways. Improved health methods before, during, and after pregnancy have lowered mortality rates in women and improved the survival rates and health of infants. These improvements include better nutrition, education about pregnancy, and general medical advances and procedures that improve the health of all involved. Among the technological advances, two areas stand out when discussing matters of reproductive health. For those attempting to avoid pregnancy, the hormone-based birth control pill has changed the sexual lives of people around the world. On the other end of the reproductive spectrum, advanced reproductive technologies (ART) such as in vitro fertilization, sperm injection, and egg donation have allowed infertile couples to have children of their own.

These advances in reproductive health have had an amazing effect on the health and well-being of women for decades. Yet for centuries, relatively little progress had been made in improving reproductive technology. One exception to this would be Charles Goodyear's process of "vulcanizing" rubber in 1844. This process allowed condoms, which had previously been made of animal skins, to be made from rubber. This change in material increased both the effectiveness of condoms in avoiding pregnancy and reduced the transmission of disease. Unlike modern condoms, which are used once and thrown away, these early rubber condoms were meant to be washed and reused.[28]

The real revolution in reproductive health occurred not in the external means of blocking pregnancy, but through an internal process. Sanger's advocacy opened public policy and legal opportunities for many women, but it was her alliance with a rich socialite, Katherine McCormick, that led to one of the greatest technological advances in reproductive health. In 1946, shortly before opening her birth control clinic, Sanger convinced McCormick to back Dr. Gregory Pincus's research into a hormone pill that would prevent pregnancies. After building on previous work and collaborations, Pincus eventually created the hormone-based birth control pill. He later worked with Dr. John Rock and the Searle pharmaceutical company to get the pill approved by the Food and Drug Administration.

While awaiting FDA approval as a form of birth control, Searle's pharmaceuticals marketed the pill for use in curing menstrual irregularities. Word soon spread of the pill's ability to stop ovulation, however, and women around the country rushed to their doctors to get it. Despite some problems with the dosage of early versions of the pill (originally the pill contained 10 times more hormone than is currently prescribed) and the side effects these high doses produced, the pill's instant popularity quickly made it the primary source of birth control for women around the country. A Johns Hopkins University study in 2007 found that 18 million women in America were using oral contraceptives.

On the other end of the reproductive-rights spectrum, medical advances have vastly improved the health of both the mother and infant throughout the pregnancy and birth process. In the early twentieth century, one in every 100 women died in or immediately following childbirth. By century's end, the number was reduced to one in every 10,000.[29] Much of this decrease is attributable to improved medical facilities dedicated to pediatric, or children's, health. Also, government agencies followed the example of European movements that focused education and health resources on improving maternal and infant mortality rates and overall health. Coupled with improved education, women and their babies are far more likely to survive the childbirth process, and then to thrive afterwards, than at any time in history.[30]

QUOTABLE

Definition of the Controversy

What are reproductive rights? According to the United Nations, in 1994:

> Reproductive rights rest on the recognition of the basic right of all couples and individuals to decide freely and responsibly the number, spacing and timing of their children and to have the information and means to do so, and the right to attain the highest standard of sexual and reproductive health. They also include the right of all to make decisions concerning reproduction free of discrimination, coercion and violence.*

The U.N. expanded this definition at a 1995 conference in Beijing:

> Reproductive health is a state of complete physical, mental and social well-being and not merely the absence of disease or infirmity, in all matters relating to the reproductive system and to its functions and processes. Reproductive health therefore implies that people are able to have a satisfying and safe sex life and that they have the capability to reproduce and the freedom to decide if, when and how often to do so. Implicit in this last condition are the right of men and women to be informed and to have access to safe, effective, affordable and acceptable methods of family planning of their choice, as well as other methods of their choice for regulation of fertility which are not against the law, and

Modern Controversies

For some people, new technology and innovations in reproductive technology are part of the progression of humanity and a benefit to everyone. These people see new forms of contraceptives as a way of relieving suffering and improving life for the people involved. They often see contraceptives as a benefit beyond the mother or immediate family, but also as a benefit to society at large since they reduce the number of unwanted pregnancies and in turn reduce the number of children who have to be cared for by the larger community. For these public

the right of access to appropriate health-care services that will enable women to go safely through pregnancy and childbirth and provide couples with the best chance of having a healthy infant. In line with the above definition of reproductive health, reproductive health care is defined as the constellation of methods, techniques and services that contribute to reproductive health and well-being by preventing and solving reproductive health problems. It also includes sexual health, the purpose of which is the enhancement of life and personal relations, and not merely counseling and care related to reproduction and sexually transmitted diseases.**

These definitions address far more than abortion and birth control. Reproductive rights are defined as including such things as being able to control how and when to have children, health before, during, and after the pregnancy, and even fulfilling sexual relationships.

*United Nations, Programme of Action adopted at the International Conference on Population and Development, Cairo, 1994. http://www.who.int/reproductive-health/gender/glossary.html.

**United Nations, Platform for Action and Beijing Declaration, Fourth World Conference on Women, September 1995. http://www.un.org/womenwatch/daw/beijing/platform/health.htm#diagnosis.

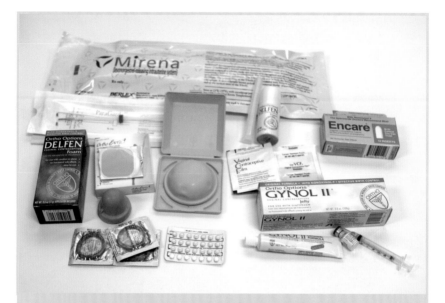

Pictured above, a display of various modern contraceptives. Although contraceptives, in one form or another, have been used to varying effect since ancient times, their widespread use and availability—particularly by minors—remains a hotly contested subject in the United States.

policy reasons, many people believe that contraceptives should be easily accessible and even free to those who need it. This may mean providing condoms in schools or free birth control pills in clinics, but the goal is always the same—to get contraceptives to those who need them.

Others do not believe contraceptives should be so widely available. Some believe that people should not have sexual relations unless they want to have children. There are those who see access to contraceptives as providing encouragement to engage in improper sexual activity, especially among minors. Many people believe that if sex is restricted to inside the marital relationship, and it is used to produce babies, then there is no need for such broad access to birth control. They also raise concerns about interfering in the natural order of things by introducing technology where nature should be left alone. Even those who do not oppose birth control for moral or ethical reasons may still oppose providing birth control for free or making it too easily accessible. They often cite the cost of such programs and their concern about government involvement in medicine.

While access to birth control is an issue of concern, the biggest debate in reproductive health remains the controversy over abortion. Whether one thinks abortion is immoral or ethical rests on the core question of when life begins. For many abortion opponents, life begins when the sperm first fertilizes the egg. For some in the abortion-rights movement, life does not begin until the fetus is viable, or able to live on its own, outside the womb. For others, the time life begins falls somewhere in between. So the debate rages on.

While the ethical argument over abortions remains, the right to an abortion has been settled law since the *Roe* decision was handed down in 1973. Most court cases today no longer question whether a woman has a right to an abortion, but instead focus on what restrictions the government can place on getting an abortion. Some states require a minor to get parental permission before getting an abortion. Other states require waiting periods before abortions can be performed. All states and the federal government place restrictions on how late in the pregnancy an abortion can be performed if there is no medical emergency (such as saving the mother's life).

The latest controversy that has sprung up around the country is what kind of sex education is appropriate in schools. While many scholars agree that improved education about reproduction has vastly improved the health of mothers and children, the debate has now focused on how much of this education do young people need, and at what age. Does the kind of education a student gets about sex affect their behavior in appropriate or inappropriate ways? These questions are being debated not only in the halls of Congress and in state legislatures, but in the schools and classrooms in every community.

The following chapters examine these three central debates in the area of reproductive rights. First, the question of access to contraceptives and what that means for those involved is discussed. Second, we turn to the controversy over abortion-related issues such as acceptable restrictions and procedures. Finally, the question of sex education in public schools is addressed.

Access to Contraceptives Should Be Liberalized

Angela faced an unexpected struggle to prevent a pregnancy after a condom broke on a Fourth of July weekend in Cleveland, Ohio. She did not have her own doctor and the local family planning clinic was closed. At 2 A.M., at the nearest hospital's emergency room, the attending physician refused to provide emergency contraception—a concentrated dose of birth control pills that can prevent a pregnancy—and he also refused to provide a referral to another source. "What should I do then?" Angela asked in a panic. The physician responded, "I don't know. You should have thought about that before." A nurse who overheard the conversation tried to help. She told Angela to contact a second hospital. But the staff there informed Angela that the hospital only offers emergency contraception to sexual assault victims. Finally, a physician at a third hospital agreed to call in a prescription to the local pharmacy. But at the pharmacy, the pharmacist told Angela that the store did not stock emergency contraception. Undeterred, Angela called the prescribing physician, who spoke with the pharmacist and convinced her to dispense the contraception.[1]

When reading Angela's tale, one is struck by the struggles she went through in order to make a responsible choice. More troubling than the particulars of this situation is what her ordeal symbolizes. In an era where women's reproductive control is central to their ability to live fulfilling and productive lives, access to contraceptives should be a matter of course. The fact that Angela had to go to three hospitals and then struggle with a pharmacist just to get the desperately needed medical care she sought demonstrates that there is still a long road ahead for the reproductive rights of women when it comes to access to contraceptives.

Contraceptives are important.

History has shown that contraceptives are an important aspect of women's health care. Throughout the ages, women have attempted to control how, when, and whether they conceive, both for their own personal advancement and for the benefit of the community. Modern medicine has provided even more insight into the benefits, both individual and corporate, of women being able to control their fertility.

Contraceptives allow women control over their reproduction. This allows women who are not financially, emotionally, physically, or otherwise ready for children to delay or completely forgo pregnancy. This control means that women have greater flexibility to determine education and career choices—providing women the same choices as men, thus equalizing the field of opportunities to make more choices accessible to more people.[2]

Beyond the direct personal benefits of controlling fertility, there are medical side benefits to some forms of birth control, especially the birth control pill. Modern birth control pills are much lower in dosage than when the pill first appeared on the market. At these new doses, birth control pills have side effects that range from cosmetic to life saving. For example, today's low dose pills have been shown to:

- Lessen acne and unwanted facial hair;
- Lessen hot flashes and other symptoms of menopause;
- Strengthen bones;
- Protect against certain cancers;
- Help prevent Pelvic Inflammatory Disease;
- Prevent pregnancy *after* sexual relations, when taken in prescribed manner.

For some women using the pill, there is also the benefit of having menstrual cycles on a regular schedule (which allows for better life planning), and can also reduce cramping and bleeding, and result in fewer symptoms of premenstrual syndrome (PMS).[3] It is for these reasons that some women take birth control pills even if they do not intend to be sexually active.

For many women, contraceptives are not just a matter of personal choice or lifestyle. They are needed treatments for managing medical conditions. And while the benefits differ at different ages, one thing is certain: Women of all ages should have the ability to get the best medical treatment available to meet their particular needs.

Age should not be a deterrent to quality medical care.

Efforts to force minors to get parental consent before getting access to birth control are harmful to both the minors and society. A woman's future prospects should be her own, and should not be overruled by third parties, not even her parents. If a woman makes a decision to engage in sexual activity, it will be her responsibility to deal with the results, whether it is a baby, a sexually transmitted disease, or relationship issues. Because the young woman will be responsible for these effects on her person, she should have as broad discretion as possible in seeking medical help.

The Supreme Court recognized this in the 1977 case of *Carey v. Population Services International.* In *Carey,* the Court determined that the state of New York could not restrict the sale of condoms to minors, and recognized a minor's right to privacy and its connection to the right to an abortion. Building on this idea of privacy, the Court found that if the state could not restrict a minor's right to an abortion by requiring parental consent, then they logically could not restrict a minor's right to birth control. Associate Justice William Brennan explained:

> Since the State may not impose a blanket prohibition, or even a blanket requirement of parental consent, on the choice of a minor to terminate her pregnancy, the constitutionality of a blanket prohibition of the distribution of contraceptives to minors is a fortiori foreclosed.[4]

Protecting the medical privacy of teenagers is essential, as illustrated by a 2005 Guttmacher Institute study. Analyzing and combining several other studies, the Guttmacher study found that parental notification would not deter teens from engaging in sexual activity, as proponents often argue. Instead, teens would still engage in sexual activity, only without effective contraception. They resort to either no birth control, or a far less effective method such as withdrawal. In these cases, the lack of birth control led to greater incidence of sexually transmitted disease and unwanted pregnancy.[5]

It is illogical to allow parental objections to defeat a teen's desire to be responsible in seeking out contraceptives. A parent's right to direct the upbringing of their child is not absolute, and as the child matures, a parent's control diminishes. In cases of Christian Science parents who do not want their children to receive medical care, the courts have routinely found that the interest in the health of the child outweighs the parent's right to control their medical access.[6] Similarly, in cases involving parental notification or consent before a minor can get an abortion, the courts have consistently held that these laws are constitutional only if they have a judicial bypass option. This option allows minors to circumvent parental involvement by seeking authorization for the abortion from a judge. In these cases, the courts recognize that going to a judge demonstrates a level of maturity proving that the minor is capable of her own decision-making. In a similar fashion, a minor who shows the maturity to seek contraceptives before engaging in sexual activity demonstrates a level of maturity that should suffice for him or her to get access to contraceptives.[7]

Gatekeepers should not be a barrier to necessary medical care.

Minors are not the only ones in danger of losing their access to contraceptives. Companies and individuals have also become an impediment to women getting the medicine they need, especially in the area of emergency contraceptives. Because of concerns by some that emergency contraceptives, or "morning-after pills," are actually a form of abortion, some pharmacies have refused to sell them. This situation was brought into sharp relief in 2005 and 2006 because of a lawsuit that gained national attention.

In December 2005, three women in three Massachusetts towns visited Wal-Mart pharmacies in an effort to fill a prescription for "Plan B," a morning-after contraceptive. Available in many pharmacies around the country, Plan B is a high dose of hormones that can be taken within five days of a sexual encounter to minimize the chances of pregnancy occurring. Wal-Mart had publicly stated that its policy was to not carry emergency contraceptives, and when the prescriptions were provided, Wal-Mart pharmacists told the women to go to one of their competitors.[8]

These women involved knew the importance of emergency contraceptives. Julie Battel is a nurse midwife. Rebekah Gee is an obstetrician/gynecologist. Katrina McCarty works for the Massachusetts Coalition Against Sexual Assault and Domestic Violence. In their professional worlds, they had seen the trials and dangers women experience when they have to deal with unwanted pregnancies. They also knew that Wal-Mart's unwillingness to provide this product in Massachusetts was not just a business decision Wal-Mart was free to make, it was a decision that broke the law.[9]

The state of Massachusetts had laws that required pharmacies to carry medications needed by communities. When Gee and the others brought their complaints to regulators in charge of pharmacy oversight, Wal-Mart was notified that its stores were required to provide Plan-B in all Massachusetts pharmacies. In the ensuing publicity over this incident, Wal-Mart publicly announced that it would provide emergency contraceptives at all of its pharmacies nationwide.[10]

Unfortunately, this was at best a partial victory. Even as more pharmacies are carrying the drugs women need, there are increasing reports of pharmacies and individual pharmacists creating additional barriers to women's access to contraceptives. Citing the First Amendment, some pharmacists claim that providing birth control violates their religious beliefs and conscience. In some cases this means that they will not serve the patient, but in other cases, it has resulted in pharmacists berating women and giving them false or misleading information about birth control.[11]

While the religious liberty of pharmacists should surely be protected, it is also important to remember that a pharmacy is a state-regulated business that agrees to serve the population according to the laws. In rural areas, women who are refused birth control at their local pharmacy may have to travel long distances to another store, which could restrict their access altogether. In urban areas, insurance companies may mandate which pharmacies must be frequented, which could raise the cost to the women if they have to go outside their insurance network to get prescriptions.[12]

Controversy over HPV Vaccine

"HPV vaccine does not promote sex, it protects women's health."[*]

In 2007, Texas Governor Rick Perry ignited a controversy when he issued an executive order mandating that all girls going into the sixth grade be immunized against the human papilloma virus (HPV), a sexually transmitted disease that can cause cancer. Within hours, officials were receiving calls from around the state from angry parents who did not want their daughters getting the vaccination. These parents argued that mandating the vaccine violated their rights as parents, and would encourage teen sex.

Advocates countered that a few shots could eradicate the cause of almost 70% of cervical cancer. Perry, a conservative who opposes abortion and stem cell research, found himself on the defensive. "Providing the HPV vaccine doesn't promote sexual promiscuity any more than providing the hepatitis B vaccine promotes drug use," Perry, a Republican, said in a prepared statement. "If the medical community developed a vaccine for lung cancer, would the same critics oppose it claiming it would encourage smoking?"[**]

Yet the controversy continued. Accusations arose that Perry was too closely tied to the manufacturer of the vaccines, Merck & Co. (Perry's former chief of staff was Merck's chief lobbyist.) The state legislature argued that the executive branch was stepping into areas that should be dealt with through legislation. Even medical associations in the state failed to support the initiative, arguing that other vaccines were more needed.

On March 14, 2007, the legislature overwhelmingly passed a bill that overrode Perry's order. On May 9, 2007, Perry said he would not veto the bill.

Currently no state has a mandated, statewide program to vaccinate girls against HPV.

[*]Catherine Paddock, "Texas Governor Perry Stands Firm on HPV Vaccination Mandate for Schoolgirls," Medical News Today, February 6, 2007. http://www.medicalnewstoday.com/articles/62417.php.

[**]Hugh Aynesworth, "Perry Defends HPV Vaccination Order," Washington Times, February 7, 2007.

In order to ensure the rights of all involved, pharmacies and the pharmacists that work in them should be required, as part of their state licensing, to make sure that policies are in place so that women can get their prescriptions filled. If pharmacists do not believe their consciences would allow them to fill a prescription, birth control or otherwise, then there should be procedures to make sure someone else can fill it at little or no inconvenience to the customer. Otherwise, an individual pharmacist could impose his or her religious or moral views on someone who may not hold similar beliefs. This is just as much a violation of religious liberty as forcing the pharmacist to provide the prescription in the first place. If the pharmacy or pharmacist is not comfortable with this arrangement, then the state should not give them the license they need to engage in business in that state.

Financial situation should not be a barrier to quality medical care.

Poverty or other financial hardship should not be a barrier to a woman's access to birth control, especially since contraceptives are one of the major ways women can overcome their financial hardships. The situation is complicated by the fact that even those with insurance do not always have the preferred method of contraception covered, if any at all. This is not just a matter of individual freedom, but of economic benefit. Insurance companies and society at large are better off paying for birth control (about $16 per person per month for birth control pills) than paying for the exponentially more expensive abortion (average $316) or pregnancy (birth alone runs between $6,000 and $80,000).[13]

Insurance companies have been slow to recognize this, and have not changed until media attention was focused on the gender disparity in insurance coverage. In particular, people were upset to learn that insurers would cover Viagra and other erectile-dysfunction medication so men could remain sexually active, but did not cover birth control pills so women could also be sexually active and protected from unwanted pregnancies. This disparity led to lawsuits and unwanted media attention.[14]

Summary

Despite abundant research demonstrating the benefits of birth control, there are still barriers to women's access to contraceptives, whether well-intentioned or otherwise. It is imperative that women have the freest access possible to the means of controlling their fertility. The benefits of such access aid not only the women involved, but also society at large. Minors must be given the freedom to make good choices about birth control, without fear of recrimination or rejection by family. Similarly, the beliefs of medical gatekeepers such as pharmacists should not be imposed on unwilling customers and patients.

While insurance companies are now covering birth control in larger numbers, there are still far too many that do not. These gaps in insurance and public policy should be closed through legislation requiring coverage for birth control and programs to provide birth control when insurance is not available.

Contraceptives Should Be Closely Monitored and Regulated

The year 2005 was a tough one for pharmacists in Illinois, especially if they happened to have moral or religious objections to contraceptives. It started in July, when a Wal-Mart pharmacy in Onalaska sought temporary help from a placement service it regularly used. The service, Medical Staffing Network, sent Neil Noesen as a contract pharmacist to the store. Before his first day, Noesen notified the store that while he was happy to work there, he was a devout Roman Catholic, and as such, it would violate his conscience and religious beliefs to help any customer with contraceptives or questions about birth control. The store assured Noesen that he would not be required to help with contraceptive counseling or filling of prescriptions.[1]

Five days later, the Onalaska store changed its stand and told Noesen that he would have to answer phone calls and refer callers

to one of the other pharmacists if the call concerned contraceptives. When Noesen refused, he was forcibly removed from the
store in a wheelchair. In a later lawsuit, the Illinois courts ruled
against Noesen, despite his having provided notice to the store
and his deep-seated desire to abide by his conscience.[2]

In November, four other pharmacists were suspended from
Walgreens stores in Illinois for refusing to fill prescriptions for
emergency contraceptives. Several other Walgreens pharmacists
filed suit over the same issue. Polls taken by ABC News found that
63 percent of polled American pharmacists thought Walgreen
Co. was wrong to suspend the four men. Other poll results indicated overwhelming support for the right of each pharmacist to
make their own decision about filling prescriptions.[3]

In each of these situations, these pharmacists' consciences
would not allow them to be involved in facilitating either abortion or the use of contraceptives. These people realize that birth
control methods are serious decisions with consequences for all
involved. That is why it is important that access to contraceptives
be monitored and closely regulated.

Contraceptives have serious consequences.

Contraceptives, especially those that involve medications or
medical procedures, are regulated by the state and for good
reason. Hormone-based birth control pills in particular have a
number of potential side effects, including

> nausea, weight gain, sore or swollen breasts, small amount
> of blood, or spotting, between periods, lighter periods
> and mood changes. . . . [Other] symptoms may indicate a
> serious disorder, such as liver disease, gallbladder disease,
> stroke, blood clots, high blood pressure, or heart disease.
> They include abdominal pain (stomach pain), chest pain,
> headaches (severe), eye problems (blurred vision) and
> swelling and/or aching in the legs and thighs.[4]

Roman Catholic Views on Reproductive Issues

In 1968, the Roman Catholic Church was shaken by controversy over a papal encyclical on birth control titled *Humanae Vitae*, or "On Human Life." Basing the pronouncement on church history and prior teachings, Pope Paul VI concluded that all forms of birth control other than the "natural" or "rhythm" method were sinful, as were all attempts at technologically assisted forms of procreation. While the document conceded that population control and family planning were important issues, it concluded that the consequences of allowing artificial methods were far worse:

> Let them consider how easily this course of action could open wide the way for marital infidelity and a general lowering of moral standards.... Another effect that gives cause for alarm is that a man who grows accustomed to the use of contraceptive methods may forget the reverence due to a woman ... reduc[ing] her to being a mere instrument for the satisfaction of his own desires.*

Worse yet, readers were warned that public authorities could force people to limit their families against their will by artificial means.

The response to this encyclical was loud and immediate. Those outside the Catholic Church criticized the teachings for ignoring science and dooming many around the world to starvation. Reactions from within the Church were even more scathing. Jesuit philosopher Norris Clarke told students at a rally at Fordham University, "You are not speaking as our Pope. We can't hear you. We demand that you do not speak to us this way."** Swiss theologian Hans Kung concluded that the pope was simply wrong. Such dissent led to weakening of the authority of the Church around the world, but particularly among American Catholics.

In May 2008, Pope Benedict XVI reaffirmed the Vatican's support for *Humanae Vitae* and the Church's position that children are to result from only the natural union of a man and woman in marriage. "No mechanical technique can substitute the act of love that two married people exchange as a sign of a greater mystery."***

*Pope Paul VI, "Consequences of Artificial Methods," *Humanae Vitae*, sec. 17.

**"The Pope and Birth Control: A Crisis in Catholic Authority," *Time*, August 9, 1968. http://www.time.com/time/magazine/article/0,9171,902263,00.html.

***Associated Press, "Pope Benedict Praises Vatican Teaching Against Birth Control," *International Herald Tribune*, May 10, 2008. http://www.iht.com/articles/ap/2008/05/10/news/Pope-Birth-Control.php.

Because of the serious nature of the pills' side effects, it is best for women to take these only when under a doctor's care. Beyond the health issues related to the pill, there are economic considerations as well. Even those who endorse making birth control pills available without a prescription recognize the economic hardship this would create for many women. Most insurance plans cover birth control pills because they are a prescription medication. If birth control pills were suddenly available over the counter, then these insurance benefits would no longer exist. This would make the cost of the pill more expensive, especially in the short term.[5]

Other forms of birth control, such as an intrauterine device (IUD), require a doctor to insert the device during an in-office procedure. In order to insert the IUD properly, a doctor has to determine the size and position of the uterus, use a speculum to hold the vagina open, stabilize the uterus with a tenaculum, and then carefully insert the IUD through the uterine opening and place it on the back wall. If done incorrectly, bleeding and infection could occur. The procedure can also cause some discomfort, and pain medications are often part of the insertion process. While this may not rise to the level of surgery, it is surely not the kind of activity that should be done by someone other than a licensed physician.[6]

Diaphragms, cervical caps, and other barrier methods also require doctor involvement and oversight. These items need to be carefully measured to make sure they are the best fit for each individual patient. Without the involvement of a doctor, these items would, at best, be less effective. The greater damage would be ineffective birth control giving women a false sense of security that results in an unplanned and possibly unwanted pregnancy.[7]

Even the most basic barrier method, condoms, should likely have some impediments to access. If people are too young or immature to go through the process of getting contraceptives, then they are too young to be engaged in sex in the first place.

State lawmakers in New York in the 1970s understood this when they attempted to require that a pharmacist distribute all contraceptives, which could not be made available to minors. Although the Supreme Court invalidated the statute for legal reasoning, the public policy ideas behind the New York law still make sense.[8]

Access to contraceptives should be a family matter.

Just as the government needs to assure that the medical community regulates birth control, it is also important that government protects individuals' privacy. When it comes to making the best decision for a minor, the government almost always defers to the wisdom of parents. This is because parents know their children far better than any generic government policy or law could, and know what each individual child needs. Because they are the ones who love and care for the child, they are most motivated to make the best decisions for their child.

This recognition of the primary place parents have in the upbringing of their children is seen in four Supreme Court decisions. The first case, which focuses on a prohibition on teaching German to students in Nebraska, may seem like an odd place for parental rights to come up. Yet in the 1923 case of *Meyer v. Nebraska*, the Supreme Court found that parents have the primary responsibility and right to control what their children learn, likening the upbringing of children to "the right of the individual to . . . engage in any of the common occupations of life . . . to marry, establish a home and bring up children, . . . and generally to enjoy those privileges long recognized at common law as essential to the orderly pursuit of happiness by free men."[9]

Two years later, another education lawsuit made its way to the Supreme Court. In *Pierce v. Society of Sisters*, a family fought to have their child attend a private school, in violation of an Oregon law that required all students to go to public school. In the end, the Court found that "[t]he child is not the mere creature of the state; those who nurture him and direct his destiny have the right, coupled with the high duty, to recognize and prepare him for additional obligations."[10] These cases show the Court's clear preference for leaving the authority of the family structure intact.

In 1944, the Supreme Court reviewed a case concerning the religious-liberty rights of parents to direct the faith of their children. The case centered on a Jehovah's Witness family that believed it was part of their religious duty for every member of the family to sell religious material. This caused a problem when 9-year-old Bettie Simmons sold religious magazines on a street corner, in violation of Massachusetts's child-labor laws. In some of the strongest wording possible, the Court explained its view of parental supremacy when it comes to decisions being made for minors:

> It is cardinal with us that the custody, care and nurture of the child reside first in the parents, whose primary function and freedom include preparation for obligations the state can neither supply nor hinder. And it is in recognition of this that these decisions have respected the private realm of family life which the state cannot enter.[11]

Finally, in a 1972 decision, the Court noted, "The history and culture of Western civilization reflect a strong tradition of parental concern for the nurture and upbringing of their children. This primary role of the parents in the upbringing of their children is now established beyond debate as an enduring American tradition."[12] The case involved Amish families who wanted to remove their children from school at the eighth grade, as had been their tradition. Wisconsin education laws required students to remain in school until they turned 16. Once again, the Court clearly followed precedent and overruled the state's interest and deferred to the parents.[13]

If the Supreme Court is so clearly willing to defer to parents when it comes to such core matters as education and religion, it follows that it should also defer to parents on matters concerning contraceptives. In both education and religion, the decisions parents make have implications for their children for the rest of their lives. In these court cases, the child's wishes were not even addressed—they were strictly matters for the parents to decide. In the same way, birth control decisions are best left to parents until the child is no longer a minor.

The rights of all involved should be protected.

It is undoubtedly important to protect a woman's right to access birth control in appropriate ways, but what some people are proposing pushes beyond protecting the rights of women and into violating the rights of others. Two areas in particular—insurance coverage for birth control and conscientious objections by doctors—have garnered recent attention.

During the 2008 presidential campaign, the question of insurance coverage for birth control caused an uncomfortable moment for Republican presidential candidate John McCain. Senator McCain was being interviewed when a question came up about the fairness of insurance companies covering Viagra (a drug that helps with erectile dysfunction) but not covering birth control. The interviewer went on to ask McCain why he voted against a bill that would require insurance companies to cover birth control. McCain stumbled uncomfortably for some time before the reporter went on and let the issue slide.[14]

This often-replayed moment brought attention to an issue that some responded to without thinking through all the implications. It seems unfair that men get coverage for drugs that enable them to have sex, yet women are not covered for things that can keep them from getting pregnant. Yet contraceptives, particularly the pill, are medicines that have some moral value attached to them. Many have come to believe that birth control pills actually cause "silent abortions." In other words, the pill may not prevent conception, but instead prevents a fertilized embryo from attaching to the uterine wall, thus causing the fertilized cells to be aborted during the next menstrual cycle. For some companies with a religious or moral stance against abortion, subsidizing these pills is a violation of their conscience. For others, even if there were no moral problem with taking the pill, there is some concern with forcing people to effectively subsidize lifestyle choices of other people. If people want to have sex without getting pregnant, then it is the couple's choice to keep that from happening. Forcing insurance companies, and eventually the people who pay for insurance, to subsidize these life choices is unfair and could lead down a slippery slope. If people are required to pay for birth control today, will they have to pay for abortions tomorrow, or perhaps even have to pay to raise someone else's child?

When it comes to insurance, some tough decisions have to be made. As Tom Wildsmith, a policy actuary for the Health Insurance Industry of America, explained, "[i]t's understandable why if you think something is important you would want someone to pay for it for you. But you can add on nice things to the point where insurance is less affordable than it is now."[15] Giving everyone everything they want eventually leads to no one getting anything they need.

Finally, discussions of rights in reproductive-health cases seldom focus on all of the parties involved. In particular, the doctors, nurses, pharmacists, and other health care employees are usually forgotten as the analysis focuses on the women seeking an abortion, contraception, etc. But health care professionals have rights, and consciences, too. They should be protected just as much as anyone else. That is exactly what some professionals are doing by raising awareness.

As the introductory story demonstrated, pharmacists and others with deeply held religious and moral convictions about birth control are often forced to make difficult decisions that can affect their futures and the welfare of their families. As Karen Brauer, head of Pharmacists for Life International, explains, "[o]ur job is to enhance life. . . . We shouldn't have to dispense a medication that we think takes lives."[16] Caroline Bollinger, in an article for *Prevention*, described a stand being taken by Dr. Cynthia Jones-Nosacek, an OB/GYN in Milwaukee:

In an interview, Jones-Nosacek, who has been in practice for 21 years, says she stopped prescribing the Pill after discovering a paper written by Salt Lake City family doctor Joseph B. Stanford, MD, an assistant professor of family and preventive medicine at the University of Utah and a recent appointee to the FDA's Reproductive Health Drugs Advisory Committee. "The paper talked about the Pill's post-fertilization effect," says Jones-Nosacek. "After reading it and several other books and papers, I realized I could no longer justify prescribing the Pill."

Although Jones-Nosacek says she may have lost patients over her stand, she thinks most are happy to hear her opinion. "I think most women feel life begins at fertilization," she says. "When they find out the Pill has a potential post-fertilization effect, they're surprised, and some rethink their decision."[17]

These professionals—and others like them—should be allowed to practice their profession without having to violate their consciences. This right is of no less value than a woman's right to access to contraceptives, so both should be protected.

Summary

Contraceptives often have side effects and need varying levels of doctor oversight and involvement. Because of the possible dangers and the implications of using birth control, it is important that these decisions be left to the family, and not interfered with by the government. It is also important that everyone's rights are protected, including those of the insurance company, the people paying into insurance, medical professionals, and the general public. Keeping in mind the consciences of all these individuals, the best policy is to keep matters of birth control private, and not subsidized by either the dollars of the insured or by the consciences of their doctors.

Abortion Should Not Be Restricted by Government or Others

"Are you judging this man, Father?"
"He has judged himself, and been found unworthy," came the cold reply.[1]

On a Sunday morning in April 2008, longtime conservative and former Reagan administration official Doug Kmiec and his wife stood in the Communion line of their church. The question rang out from the back of the line, and the priest's response was directed at Kmiec, who stood before the priest with outstretched hands. Kmiec was being denied Communion that morning in response to his actions the week before. That week, Kmiec "had cooperated with evil ... had killed babies ... [his] heart was black ... [he gave] scandal to the entire church." During the morning homily, the priest decried Kmiec's actions as those that, "[n]o faithful Catholic would ever contemplate doing," thus making Kmiec, "dead to the Holy Mother Church."[2]

What had Doug Kmiec, a conservative, "pro-life," Catholic advocate and scholar, done to earn such ignominy? The week before he had endorsed Barack Obama in the 2008 presidential campaign. The reason this was so distressing to Kmiec's priest was that Obama had stated that he supported protecting a woman's right to choose when it came to issues of abortion.[3]

Kmiec's parish priest was not alone. After election day, the Reverend Jay Scott Newman wrote to his parishioners at St. Mary's Catholic Church that those who had voted for President-elect Obama would put their immortal souls at risk if they took Communion without first doing penance for their vote. In his letter, he explained:

> Our nation has chosen for its chief executive the most radical pro-abortion politician ever to serve in the United States Senate or to run for president. . . . Voting for a pro-abortion politician when a plausible pro-life alternative exists constitutes material cooperation with intrinsic evil, and those Catholics who do so place themselves outside of the full communion of Christ's Church and under the judgment of divine law. Persons in this condition should not receive Holy Communion until and unless they are reconciled to God in the Sacrament of Penance, lest they eat and drink their own condemnation.[4]

It is important to support a woman's right to an abortion.

In his book *The Audacity of Hope*, Obama explained that he supports a woman's right to choose based on both pragmatic and ideological reasons. From the pragmatic side, if abortion is made illegal, women will be put at risk because abortions will be done illegally, which leads to unsafe abortions. Ideologically, Obama argues that women do not make this choice lightly, and that he trusts women to make their own choices without the government's interference.[5]

Obama's approach reflects the beliefs of millions of other Americans. For these people, a woman's right to an abortion also rests not on a single rationale, but on both ideological and pragmatic grounds. From an ideological standpoint, many people are offended by the idea that governments should tell women what they can and cannot do with their bodies. Paternalistic views promoted by abortion opponents, and in some cases justices on the Supreme Court, demonstrate a desire to save women from themselves.[6] Each time a government "protects" women by making decisions for her, all women's liberty is diminished.

QUOTABLE

Abortion in the Bible

When people who are fighting injure a pregnant woman so that there is a miscarriage, and yet no further harm follows, the one responsible shall be fined what the woman's husband demands, paying as much as the judges determine. If any harm follows, then you shall give life for life, eye for eye, tooth for tooth, hand for hand, foot for foot, burn for burn, wound for wound, stripe for stripe.
Exodus 21:22–25 (New Revised Standard Version)

In the Jewish Torah and the Christian Bible, abortion is only mentioned once, in the Book of Exodus. The author explains that if a pregnant woman who is struck during a dispute loses the child she is carrying, then the perpetrator of the crime is required to pay a monetary damage. Despite what some Christian and Jewish groups may claim, the only mention of abortion in the Bible is described as a simple assault, not an act of murder. The passage speaks only of harm to the mother, with no mention of the fetus as being alive or independent in any way. In fact, some further harm to the mother is required before the law of Lex Talonis ("eye for an eye and tooth for a tooth")—the law used when physical harm is involved—is even invoked. This has caused some Christians and Jews to reject the claims that their faith requires an anti-abortion stance and instead clears the way for more "pro-choice" stances.

Whenever liberty is diminished, the ability for one to be a full citizen is diminished. As Justice Ruth Bader Ginsburg explained in her dissent in *Gonzales v. Carhart*:

> Women, it is now acknowledged, have the talent, capacity, and right "to participate equally in the economic and social life of the Nation." . . . Their ability to realize their full potential, the Court recognized, is intimately connected to "their ability to control their reproductive lives." . . . . Thus, legal challenges to undue restrictions on abortion procedures do not seek to vindicate some generalized notion of privacy; rather, they center on a woman's autonomy to determine her life's course, and thus to enjoy equal citizenship stature.[7]

Another ideological element of supporters of a woman's right to choose rests on the medical reality of the situation. An abortion removes cells from a woman's body before these cells form into a child. A clump of four, 16, 32, or 1,000 cells do not constitute a human life. These cells, especially early in the pregnancy, cannot live on their own. What anti-abortion groups advocate is really the position that society should deprive a woman of control over her body in exchange for protecting cells. Exchanging a real person's freedoms and liberties for a potential person's is not a decision many women are willing to make. Similarly, even many people who would never consider having an abortion still agree that it is not the government's job to make that decision for others.[8]

In any event, a fetus is not legally considered a full person, but at best, a potential person.[9] Therefore, the accusation that abortion is murder are unfounded. The woman, who is a legally recognized person, is the one who endures the difficulties of pregnancy. The stress that pregnancy puts on a woman's body alters her physiology. Given the potential damage pregnancy does to a woman, surely women have the right to protect themselves from such danger and damage. No one would blame a woman for protecting herself from an attacker in a dark alley who could leave her with permanent damage to her body. So why should women be less able to protect themselves from internal attacks as well?[10]

There is a libertarian argument against the anti-abortion position.

The weakness of anti-abortion arguments is most clearly seen by their inconsistency, especially when it comes to violence. While claiming to be pro-life, those on the fringes of the movement approve of—and in some cases have participated in—the murder of doctors who perform abortions. The fact that these people resort to violence and murder demonstrates the weakness of their arguments. If their position was true and in the best interest of the country, then they could present it in the marketplace of ideas and allow people to come to their own conclusions. Since they have been unable to win people to their position through democratic means, some have resorted to the violent terrorism seen in the late 1980s and early 1990s, where abortion clinics and their staffs were bombed, assaulted, and assassinated.[11]

Similarly, others in the movement have advocated for coercive laws that restrict a woman's rights in an effort to enforce their own morality. If they could convince women of the truth of their positions, there would be no need to push for these laws. While abortion-rights advocates have pushed for legal protection for women, there has been no corresponding push in the anti-abortion movement. The assurance that their arguments will carry them when violence will not shows one of the strengths of the abortion-rights movement's positions.[12]

Pragmatic arguments for keeping abortion legal focus less on the debate over the life status of the fetus and looks to the concrete realities that history demonstrates exist around abortion. One of the biggest issues for many people who are concerned about the health and welfare of women is the danger that outlawing abortions will not stop abortions, but merely make them illegal and unsafe. Estimates range from 200,000 to 1.3 million abortions being performed illegally in

Timeline of Abortion-Related Cases Before the U.S. Supreme Court

1971—*United States v. Vuich*, 402 U.S. 62: The Supreme Court upholds Washington, D.C., law that allows for abortion to preserve a mother's life or health.

1973—*Roe v. Wade*, 410 U.S. 113: The Court determines that a woman has a right to an abortion during the first trimester of the pregnancy, but that the state has an interest in regulating abortion after the first trimester, and a compelling interest in the pregnancy once the fetus became viable.

1976—*Planned Parenthood v. Danforth* 428 U.S. 52: The Court finds that states cannot outlaw certain methods of abortion nor can they require a married woman to get her husband's consent before an abortion, but they can require minors to get parental consent as long as judicial bypass options are available.

1977—*Maher v. Doe*, 432 U.S. 526: The Court determines there is no right to state funding for abortions, even if indigent women are covered for other pregnancy items.

1979—*Bellotti v. Baird*, 443 U.S. 622: The Court overturns parental notification and consent laws where no judicial bypass is available.

1980—*Harris v. McRae,* 448 U.S. 297: The Court upholds Hyde Amendment that restricts federal funding for abortions.

1983—*Akron v. Akron Center for Reproductive Health*, 462 U.S. 416: The Court strikes down laws restricting abortion in the first trimester.

the United States during the late 1940s to early 1950s.[13] These were unregulated, often at the hands of inexperienced and poorly equipped abortionists in unhealthy environments. This caused numerous women to become sick and sometimes die

---

1986—*Thornburgh v. American College of Obstetricians and Gynecologists,* 476 U.S. 477: The Court overturns a state law requiring abortions to be conducted in a way most likely to allow for a live fetus.

1989—*Webster v. Reproductive Health Services,* 492 U.S. 490: The Court finds state facilities are not required to perform abortions.

1990—*Ohio v. Akron Center for Reproductive Health,* 497 U.S. 502; *Hodgson v. Minnesota,* 497 U.S. 417: The Court finds parental notification is constitutional as long as there is a judicial bypass option.

1991—*Rust v. Sullivan,* 500 U.S. 173: The Court upholds a ban on federal funding for abortion counseling.

1992—*Planned Parenthood v. Casey,* 505 U.S. 833: The Court upholds *Roe,* but rejects the trimester model, focusing instead on viability.

1994—*Madsen v. Women's Health Center,* 512 U.S. 753: The Court upholds buffer zones around abortion clinics.

1997—*Schenk v. Pro-Choice Network,* 519 U.S. 357: The Court upholds fixed buffer zones, but strikes down "floating" buffer zones as an unconstitutional infringement on free speech.

2006—*Stenberg v. Carhart,* 530 U.S. 914: The Court overturns Nebraska's ban on "partial-birth" abortions.

2006—*Ayotte v. Planned Parenthood of Northern New England,* 546 U.S. 320: The Court finds notification and wait laws must include a provision for medical emergency or are unconstitutional.

2007—*Gonzales v. Carhart* and *Gonzales v. Planned Parenthood Federation of America,* 127 S. Ct. 1610: The Court upholds federal ban on "partial-birth" abortions.

Supporters and opponents of abortion rights stand before the Supreme Court in Washington, D.C. in 2006 to mark the thirty-third anniversary of the *Roe v. Wade* decision that legalized abortion in America.

from poorly performed procedures. In contrast, since abortions have been legalized, it is one of the safest procedures, with little history of complication or side effects. Recent studies have also refuted many of the claims made by abortion opponents, including the claim that abortions lead to depression, cancer, and sterility.[14]

A ban on abortion is not the only danger to a woman's health. Even laws that discourage abortions or impede a woman's access can cause harm. By waiting later in the pregnancy, the danger to the woman increases and is often more stressful and expensive.[15] Another often-ignored aspect of criminalizing abortion is the idea of forcing women to care for an unwanted child. If a poor decision led to the pregnancy in the first place, how much worse will the decisions be when they are being made for the baby who will have to live with the consequences? Ultimately, someone too immature or otherwise not ready for a child could harm the child or end up leaving the child as a burden to the system. For abortion opponents who argue that adoption is always an option, it should be remembered that while there are people in line to adopt healthy babies from preferred racial groups, the system is filled with babies who are not healthy or otherwise not "preferred" for adoption. Many of these children also end up with problems later in life, as do the mothers who were forced to bear them.[16]

"Pro-life" activists should not prevent women from getting an abortion.

Because the Supreme Court has reiterated that women have the right to abort a nonviable fetus, the question for many women now is whether they have the access to that right. The barriers to a woman's right to choose has come under attack by private, anti-abortion groups as well as local, state, and federal governments.

Beginning in the 1980s and into the 1990s, organizations such as Operation Rescue began a strategy of "rescue." This strategy involved acts of civil disobedience ranging from trespassing and disturbing the peace to assault and arson in an attempt to block access to and halt the operations of abortion clinics. For some women, these actions effectively denied them the opportunity to exercise their right to an abortion. This led to situations where officials could not, and in many cases would not, protect women as they tried to get in to see a doctor.

Ultimately, these tactics required federal intervention through the use of special laws designed to make blocking access to a clinic a federal crime.[17] In 1994, Congress passed the Freedom of Access to Clinic Entrances Act that made it a federal crime to block or interfere with people seeking access to a clinic. This act faced numerous challenges, and remained intact in almost all areas. (The one section of the act that the Supreme Court did strike down was the idea of a "floating buffer zone" around people who were traveling toward a clinic.) Today, however, this federal law requires that protesters not interfere with people attempting to access a clinic for the purpose of getting an abortion.[18]

Some have argued that such actions have limited the free-speech rights of abortion protesters. It is true that abortion protesters are limited in exercising their rights, but it is also important to remember that even the right to free speech is not absolute. Yelling "fire" in a crowded theater when no such fire exists is not protected speech.[19] The courts have recognized that while the First Amendment protects a person's right to free speech, that right stops where another person's right starts. Therefore, while abortion protesters have the right to speak out against abortion, they do not have the right to do so in a way that interferes with a woman's right to get an abortion.[20]

Government should not interfere with a woman's choice.

It is not always private organizations that attempt to limit a woman's right to access an abortion. In some cases, the government creates some of the biggest barriers for women. At the end of 2008, 24 states had mandatory waiting periods between when a woman discussed an abortion with her doctor and when the abortion occurs. These laws typically mandate a 24-hour wait, although some states' waiting periods are longer.[21] Seventeen states mandate counseling before a woman can get an abortion, and four states do not permit insurance coverage for an abortion unless the mother's life is in danger. Yet possibly the most troubling are the 34 states that require parental notification and/or consent before a minor can get an abortion.

These laws can be devastating to a young woman, especially in cases in which the abortion is the result of incest, or in cases in which physical abuse is present. Such notification laws effectively exclude some young women from exercising their rights. Instead of discouraging young women from abortions, these laws instead encourage these minors to evade the law, travel to a state with more relaxed abortion restrictions, or seek an illegal abortion.[22]

In an even more troubling trend for abortion rights of minors, the Supreme Court has changed direction on one of the foundational pieces of abortion rights protection. Before 2007, the high court consistently required any restriction on abortions to include exceptions in cases of medical emergency or the health of the mother. The case of *Gonzalez v. Carhart* changed that. In *Carhart*, the Court found that some abortion restrictions do not have to have a provision that allows abortions in cases of medical emergency.[23]

This is a slippery slope. If the Court extends the same logic to notification laws, minors seeking abortions could be placed in danger if laws are passed that do not include emergency exceptions. In these instances, laws designed to preserve the potential life of a fetus may ultimately cost that potential life as well as the actual life of the woman carrying the fetus.

Summary

Abortion is a private matter, best left to the people most directly affected—a woman and her healthcare provider. The future of women's rights over their bodies, however, is in question. Changes on the Supreme Court and in legislation around the country could easily chip away at women's rights until the right to an abortion is a rule engulfed by exceptions.

Today, *Roe* is still the law of the land. In their 2001 book on the topic of *Roe*, N.E.H. Hull and Peter Charles Hoffer explained:

> *Roe* still stands because it symbolized an idea whose time had come—the idea that women's bodies belong

to women, not men, not doctors, not pressure groups, not Congress, not lobbyists, and certainly not judges and justices in court.[24]

If *Roe* continues to stand, it will be through the hard work of citizens intent on protecting women's right to control their own bodies. If Americans fail to stand up for such basic rights for women, history and current practice show that governments and pressure groups are more than willing to step in and remove that control from women once again.

Abortion Should Be Heavily Regulated and Eventually Outlawed

In March 2008, Health and Human Services Secretary Michael Levitt became concerned over ethics standards for doctors who specialize in obstetrics and gynecology. Specifically, he felt that the rules introduced in 2007—requiring board-certified doctors to refer a patient to another doctor if they were unwilling to perform an abortion—violated federal regulations that protected doctors who worked at federally funded institutions from discrimination. These rules provided discrimination protection for doctors who refused to violate their conscience by referring a person to another doctor for the purpose of getting an abortion. So Levitt wrote a letter to the certification board and the college of medicine that outlined his concerns:

> I am concerned that the actions taken by ACOG [the American College of Obstetricians and Gynecologists] and ABOG [the American Board of Obstetrics and

Gynecology] could result in the denial or revocation of Board certification of a physician who—but for his or her refusal, for example, to refer a patient for an abortion— would be certified. These actions, in turn, could result in certain HHS-funded State and local governments, institutions, or other entities that require Board certification taking action against the physician based just on the Board's denial or revocation of certification. In particular, I am concerned that such actions by these entities would violate federal laws against discrimination.[1]

This situation caused Levitt and former President George W. Bush to become troubled that the medical community was either not aware, or was not respecting, the strongly held beliefs that some people had over the issue of abortion. In response, the Bush administration began hearings on new regulations for the Department of Health and Human Services that would reinforce and remind the medical community of the laws protecting doctors who would neither perform abortions nor refer a patient to a doctor who would. According to Levitt, "Doctors and other health care providers should not be forced to choose between good professional standing and violating their conscience.... This rule protects the right of medical providers to care for their patients in accord with their conscience."[2]

Thus the perennial conflict over abortion continues. For those who believe that abortion is wrong, this is a matter of conscience that is not likely to be resolved any time soon. In fact, for many who believe abortion is murder, the issue of abortion is truly one of life and death.

There are several core arguments against abortion.
The debate over abortion has raged for decades, although it is only in the past 40 years that the controversy has gained so much national attention. Arguments against abortion focus on the following:

- The fetus is a living human being.
- Killing this human being denies that child the right to exist and contribute.
- Abortion denies society the possible benefits this child could produce.
- Families eager for a child are denied the option of adopting the unwanted child.
- Abortions physically and emotionally harm the mother and father.
- Abortions are an inefficient means of birth control.
- Abortions violate a doctor's Hippocratic oath to do no harm.
- A widespread use of abortions can lead down the slippery slope of unethical reproductive decisions as advanced genetic testing becomes a reality.[3]

While some of these reasons carry more weight than others, they have all been used to explain why abortion should be banned. The Supreme Court's 1973 *Roe v. Wade* decision established that a woman's constitutional right to privacy included a right to an abortion. Since that time, those who oppose abortion have changed tactics, though not the goal. Now the above arguments are used to limit the availability of abortions and restrict when and how abortions can be performed during a pregnancy. While the immediate goal is to limit abortion whenever possible, the protection and sanctity of human life requires that the ultimate goal be to ban abortion in all forms.

There is no question as to when life begins.

Of the arguments against abortion, the common denominator is ultimately a question of when life begins. The abortion debate looks far different if a person considers the fetus inside the mother a blob of cells than if that fetus is considered a baby. For many people, life begins either at the moment of conception or sometime during the gestation period. Since abortion always removes and kills the fetus, abortion always involves taking the life of another.

One group of ancient Greek philosophers, the Pythagoreans, recognized that a life was created at the moment of conception. For Pythagoreans, the soul was activated and placed in the fetus along with the full code of humanity at that very moment of conception. The philosopher Plato also discussed in his writings about the human soul and reincarnation that souls transfer at the moment of conception.[4] Laws in the ancient world also outlawed abortion, thus recognizing the value of the life that was being extinguished.[5]

Today, many theologians, philosophers, and medical doctors agree that life begins either at conception or shortly thereafter and are therefore against abortion. The Catholic Church has long held to the belief that no one can truly know when a fetus becomes a living person, and, therefore, everyone should act as though it occurs at the moment of conception.[6] This is the only way to be sure that the potential killing of another person is avoided. Other Christian groups are more emphatic. Evangelicals in particular have long held that life begins at conception and therefore abortion is always an evil. This issue even led many in Evangelical churches to become politically active during the 1980s.[7] The Islamic faith also considers abortion wrong, with the level of evil it represents increasing as the pregnancy progresses.[8] Jewish thought is more diverse, though many Orthodox Jews are clearly against the practice.[9]

Modern medicine has also indicated that life begins within the womb, with some texts pointing to conception as the start of life. One required text for many medical students is *Human Embryology and Teratology* by William James Larson. In it, he explains, "Fertilization is an important landmark because, under ordinary circumstances, a new, genetically distinct human organism is thereby formed."[10]

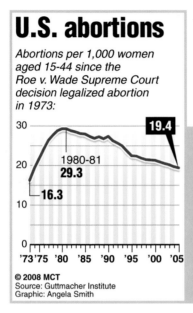

U.S. abortions

Abortions per 1,000 women aged 15-44 since the Roe v. Wade Supreme Court decision legalized abortion in 1973:

1980-81
29.3

16.3

19.4

'73 '75 '80 '85 '90 '95 '00 '05

© 2008 MCT
Source: Guttmacher Institute
Graphic: Angela Smith

This line chart shows the abortion rate in the United States between 1973 and 2005. Although abortions rose steadily until the early 1980s, the widespread use of the procedure has been on the decline since that time.

Government leaders have also begun to recognize the reality of life in the womb. In 2004, former President Bush signed into law the Unborn Victims of Violence Act, which recognizes unborn children as victims if they are injured during the commission of certain types of crimes. This recognition indicates that even inside the womb, the fetus has legal status independent from the mother.[11] Thirty-five states also have laws that recognize an unborn child as a separate victim if injured during the commission of a crime.[12]

States have a right and a duty to protect citizens.

While under *Roe v. Wade* and other Supreme Court decisions a woman has a right to an abortion, these decisions do not relieve the state of its responsibility to protect its citizens. According to *Roe*, a pregnancy can be divided into three parts, and the government's ability to regulate abortion is different at each of these three stages. During the first trimester, a woman

Proposed Amendments to the U.S. Constitution to Prohibit Abortion

Since *Roe v. Wade*, attempts have been made to amend the Constitution in order to make abortion illegal. Below are three proposed amendments that did not pass.

Human Life Amendment (1973)

Section 1: With respect to the right to life, the word "Person" as used in this article and in the Fifth and Fourteenth Articles of Amendment to the Constitution of the United States applies to all human beings irrespective of age, health, function, or condition of dependency, including their unborn offspring at every stage of their biologic development.

Section 2: No unborn person shall be deprived of life by any person; provided, however, that nothing in this article shall prohibit a law permitting only those medical procedures required to prevent the death of the mother.

Section 3: The Congress and the several States shall have power to enforce this article by appropriate legislation.

The Paramount Amendment (1979)

The paramount right to life is vested in each human being from the moment of fertilization without regard to age, health, or condition of dependency.

Unity Human Life Amendment (1981)

Section 1: The right to life is a paramount and most fundamental right of a person.

Section 2: With respect to the right to life guaranteed to persons by the Fifth and Fourteenth Articles of Amendment to the Constitution, the word "person" applies to all human beings, irrespective of age, health, function, or condition of dependency, including their unborn offspring at every state of their biological development including fertilization.

Section 3: No unborn person shall be deprived of life by any person; provided, however, that nothing in this article shall prohibit a law allowing justification to be shown for only those medical procedures required to prevent the death of either the pregnant woman or her unborn offspring as long as such law requires every reasonable effort be made to preserve the life of each.

Section 4: Congress and the several States shall have power to enforce this article by appropriate legislation.

Source: http://www.humanlifeamendment.info/.

has a right to an abortion and the state must show a compelling government interest before interfering with this right. After the first trimester, the state may regulate abortions if they can show that the regulations are reasonably related to maternal health. Finally, the state can regulate and even completely outlaw abortions after the fetus has reached viability, as long as there is an exception for the protection of the mother's life.[13] As a result of *Roe*, the laws in 46 states had to be modified to meet the new requirements.

Pennsylvania's state Legislature modified the state's abortion law in 1988 and 1989 in an attempt to comply with the new standards and better regulate abortions. These rules included five new provisions that were particularly controversial and eventually led to a lawsuit. The Pennsylvania Abortion Control Act mandated

> that a woman seeking an abortion give her informed consent prior to the procedure, and specifies that she be provided with certain information at least 24 hours before the abortion is performed; ... mandates the informed consent of one parent for a minor to obtain an abortion, but provides a judicial bypass procedure; ... commands that, unless certain exceptions apply, a married woman seeking an abortion must sign a statement indicating that she has notified her husband; ... defines a "medical emergency" that will excuse compliance with the foregoing requirements; and ... impose[s] certain reporting requirements on facilities providing abortion services.[14]

A group of doctors and abortion clinics sued over these provisions, claiming that they interfered with women's right to an abortion. The state of Pennsylvania argued that *Roe* was unworkable, and should be overturned. While the Supreme Court refused to overturn *Roe*, it still found for the state on most points.[15] The Court did this by rejecting the rigid three phases of a pregnancy model and instead created a new rule.[16] Under this new rule, the state has discretion to create laws regulating or even forbidding all abortions of viable fetuses. While a woman still has a right to abort a nonviable fetus, the Court found that the state could regulate abortions as long as the state does not create an "undue burden" on the woman's ability to exercise her rights. The Court explained that an "undue burden" is a "substantial obstacle in the path of a woman seeking an abortion of a nonviable fetus."[17]

Using this standard, the Court examined the various rules questioned by the doctors in this case. First, the Court examined the issue of informed consent and a 24-hour waiting period.

Religious Views Against Abortion

Catholicism—The head of the Catholic Church, Pope Benedict XVI, stated in 2008: "The Church's ethical judgment concerning abortion and divorce is clear and well-known to everyone: they are grave sins which—in various ways and with due evaluation of subjective responsibilities—injure the dignity of the human person, involve a profound injustice in human and social relationships, and offend God Himself, the guarantor of the marital bond and the architect of life."*

Reform Judaism—The Talmud, a sacred text of rabbinical law dating from the first half of the first century A.D., states that an abortion is acceptable only when the mother's life is in danger. It can be performed "as late as the moment before the head of a baby emerges from the birth canal," according to the Web site of the Union for Reform Judaism. Reform goes beyond that dictate to include rape, incest, diseases and severe disability revealed through genetic testing, the belief by parents that caring for a child would be impossible, and other circumstances.

Pentecostalism—David Jackson, spokesman for the United Pentecostal Church International, said the Church opposes legalized abortion and calls it "the corporate sin of abortion." Pentecostals believe life begins at conception. Believers pray for the nation to undergo a "spiritual awakening" from a culture of "permissive sexuality" and are directed to provide counseling for women dealing with

Writing for the plurality, Justice Sandra Day O'Connor repeatedly explained that there is no constitutional violation when the state requires a person seeking a medical procedure to be provided information and that person to make an informed decision about the procedure they are to undertake. Similarly, having to wait 24 hours for the information to be digested and thought through was also not considered an undue burden because "the idea that important decisions will be more informed and deliberate if they follow some period of reflection does not strike us as unreasonable. . . . In theory, at least, the waiting period is a reasonable measure to implement the State's interest in protecting the life of the unborn, a measure that does not amount to an undue burden."[18]

an unwanted pregnancy and for those who have previously had an abortion. The organization runs an adoption agency and children's homes in that vein.

Buddhism—In a 1993 interview in the *New York Times*, the Dalai Lama said, "Of course, abortion, from a Buddhist viewpoint, is an act of killing and is negative, generally speaking. But it depends on the circumstances. If the unborn child will be retarded or if the birth will create serious problems for the parent, these are cases where there can be an exception. I think abortion should be approved or disapproved according to each circumstance."

Islam—Imam Nabeel Khan from the Islamic Center of Central Missouri said abortion is not allowed in the Muslim faith except in circumstances when the mother's life is in danger, the child is known to suffer from severe disease or disability, or the pregnancy was a result of incest or rape. The abortion must be performed within 120 days—the day on which Muslims believe the soul enters the body—or it is considered a grave sin. He added that this view is that of more mainstream Muslims and that religious scholars vary on their opinion of when abortion is permissible.**

*Universal Press International. "Pope Calls Divorce, Abortion, 'Grave Sins.'" April 8, 2008. http://www.arcamax.com/religionandspirituality/s-330191-100894.

**Annie Nelson, "Religious Views on Abortion." *Columbia Tribune*. March 3, 2007. http://www.columbiatribune.com/2007/Mar/20070303Feat002.asp.

The issue of parental consent for minors was also found to be a reasonable, constitutionally allowed restriction. The Court referred to earlier cases such as *Akron II* and *Hodgson*, where they had already found these laws to be constitutionally valid as long as they included a bypass provision. Such provisions allow minors to go to a judge to get permission if parental consent is unreasonable or too much of a burden. Since judicial bypass was included in the law, the parental consent provision was also found constitutional in this case.[19]

Similarly, in both the definition of "medical emergency" and in the reporting requirements for abortion clinics, the Court found no constitutional impediment. In both instances, the Court found that defining medical emergencies and requiring good record keeping were not undue burdens, but instead were reasonable elements of a law that were related to a woman's health.[20]

The only issue in which where the Court found in favor of Planned Parenthood and the doctors who were appealing was in the matter of spousal notification. The Court examined information concerning the prevalence of spousal abuse and coercion, and concluded that if a woman had to tell her husband she was getting an abortion, there were many instances where this would not only be an undue burden, but also would substantially limit a woman's ability to get an abortion. Therefore, the Court struck down this part of Pennsylvania's abortion code.[21]

In response to the *Casey* decision, many states have attempted a variety of means to protect the life of the unborn, as well as the health of the mother. At the end of 2008, 34 states required minors to involve their parents in some way before getting an abortion, either through parental consent or notification requirements. Twenty-four states required women to undergo a waiting period before getting an abortion, and 17 states required pre-abortion counseling. Thirty-eight states required a licensed physician perform all abortions.[22]

States have also found ways to make sure those who oppose abortion are also protected. For instance, 46 states and the federal government have provisions that allow doctors to refuse to participate in abortions. Funding of abortions is also an issue. As of early 2009, 32 states have various restrictions on the use of public funds for abortions. In each instance, states have recognized the problems with abortion and the issues many people have related to it. In response they have provided ways to keep doctors and taxpayers from participating if it violates the dictates of their conscience.[23]

Summary

While abortion is considered a right that must be protected from state interference in some instances, that may change in the future. As many scholars have pointed out, new justices appointed to the Supreme Court may be more open to reexamining *Roe* and the question of abortion. Chief Justice John Roberts and Associate Justice Samuel Alito, two recent appointees, are both considered more conservative justices, and some have speculated that they will be involved in changing, if not help completely overruling, *Roe* and *Casey* in the near future.[24] Until then, it will be up to states and grassroots organizations to carry on their anti-abortion efforts.

Schools Should Provide Students with Comprehensive Sex Education

I n fall 2001, a 15-year-old girl stood with a group of other teens in a church in Lubbock, Texas. In unison, these teenagers pledged to friends and family, "On my wedding night, that will be my first time." Shelby Knox took this vow as part of her religious upbringing as a Southern Baptist. While this event was meaningful to her from a religious perspective, she became troubled when the pastor who administered the oath to her and her friends at church showed up at school to provide a secularized version for students there. In Lubbock, this "abstinence until marriage" approach was the only sex education the students were to receive. Knox became even more concerned when she found that Lubbock had one of the highest rates of teen pregnancy and of sexually transmitted infections (STIs) in the country. When she tried to get the school board to change from an abstinence-until-marriage curriculum to a more comprehensive approach, she was shut down. This started Shelby on a seven-year quest to change sex education away from abstinence only to a comprehensive approach that provides information about safe-sex practices and birth control.[1]

In a study released on December 29, 2008, Johns Hopkins University researcher Janet E. Rosenbaum analyzed sexual-behavior data of teenagers collected by the federal government. Rosenbaum first matched data based on 100 shared characteristics, including similar religious viewpoints, political outlooks and views on sex. She found that when students who took abstinence (or "virginity") pledges were compared with students who did not, there was no difference in whether they waited until marriage to have sex. In fact, the only difference between the two groups was that the students who took abstinence pledges were 10 points less likely to use birth control or safe-sex practices.[2] This report strengthened previous analysis by using stringent research and statistical techniques designed to remove other factors that could have influenced a student's sexual decisions. For advocates of comprehensive sex education, these studies validate the belief that abstinence-only techniques, such as the virginity pledges examined in Rosenbaum's study, do not work. Worse, they put young people at risk of disease and unwanted pregnancy.[3]

Abstinence-only education is ineffective and dangerous.

The modern abstinence movement began in 1981 under President Ronald Reagan. The Adolescent Family Life Act used $11 million of federal money to discourage teen pregnancy by "promoting chastity and self discipline."[4] Abstinence programs were given more funding in the administration of President Bill Clinton as part of welfare-reform initiatives. Yet the biggest boost in funding occurred during George W. Bush's presidency, when hundreds of millions of dollars were given in block grants to the states to fund abstinence-only programs in schools. Combined, taxpayers have spent $1.5 billion on abstinence-only sex education.[5]

Despite their generous funding, these programs do not work and often have unintended consequences, as several studies have shown. In 2004, a congressional study of these federally funded programs found many were riddled with inaccurate information and focused on scaring teenagers instead of educating them. The study researchers found that "over 80% of the abstinence-only curricula, used by over two-thirds of [federally funded] grantees in 2003, contain false, misleading, or distorted information

QUOTABLE

Excerpts from the Testimony of Shelby Knox before the U.S. House Committee on Oversight and Government Reform, April 23, 2008

I was born and raised in a Southern Baptist family in Lubbock, Texas—a city with some of the highest rates of teen pregnancy and sexually transmitted infections in the nation. At fifteen, in accordance with my faith, I took a virginity pledge as part of a ceremony at my church. Even though I was well past puberty, I still held an embarrassingly vague notion of the physiological definition of the act we were told to avoid. The pastor reiterated throughout the virginity pledge discussion how disappointed our parents, church, and future spouse would be if we relinquished our virginity before marriage....

While purity pledges were first the domain of religious abstinence-only programs presented in churches, they have gained popularity in secular, school-based abstinence-only programs in recent years.... New research has shown that this component is not only ineffective, but may actually be harmful because they undermine contraceptive use and inadvertently promote risky oral and anal sex among teens who see these activities as a "loophole" in their pledge.

A study done on the virginity pledges found that teenagers who sign a pledge do delay sexual activity eighteen months longer than their peers who did not pledge—far short of marriage—but are one-third less likely to use contraception upon initiating sexual activity than students about reproductive health."[6] These inaccuracies included misrepresenting the effectiveness of condoms and false information about the risks associated with abortion.[7]

These abstinence-only programs have also not been effective. After more than a quarter century of federal funding for these programs, teen pregnancy and sexually transmitted infections are still high in America. The United States has one of the highest rates of teen pregnancy among industrialized nations, 22 percent as compared with 4 percent in Sweden.[8] Worse yet, 2006 saw the first increase in teen pregnancies in 15 years.[9]

who did not pledge.[*] Students who pledged also have the same rates of sexually transmitted infections as their non-pledging peers, but are less likely to seek testing or treatment for a sexually transmitted infection.[**] In addition, male and female pledgers are six times more likely to engage in oral sex than peers who have not pledged, and male pledgers are four times more likely to engage in anal sex than their non-pledging contemporaries....

It is a perilous and confusing time to be young in the United States: just this year the CDC announced that teen birth rates are up for the first time in sixteen years and that one in four teen girls has a sexually transmitted infection....

As a young person with firsthand experience about the misinformation, shame, guilt, and intolerance propagated by these programs, I urge you to eliminate funding for abstinence-only-until-marriage programs and instead to allocate those funds to comprehensive, medically accurate sex education that provides young people with the tools they need to make responsible, informed decisions about their sexual health.[***]

Source: http://oversight.house.gov/documents/20080423120409.pdf.

[*]Peter Bearman and Hanah Brückner, "Promising the Future: Virginity Pledges and the Transition to First Intercourse," *American Journal of Sociology.* 106, no. 4 (2001): pp. 859–912.

[**]Peter Bearman and Hanah Brückner, "After the promise: The STD consequences of adolescent virginity pledges," *Journal of Adolescent Health.* 36, no. 4 (2005): pp. 271–278.

[***]Ibid.

Sexual health is not much better, as a 2008 Centers for Disease Control and Prevention study found that one in four teenage girls in America had a sexually transmitted infection.[10] In 2007, Mathematica Policy research conducted a study that found abstinence-only programs were no more successful in getting teenagers to abstain than if they had no sex education. A similar study by the Society for Adolescent Medicine found "the efficacy of abstinence-only interventions may approach zero."[11]

One key component in abstinence education has also raised particular concerns: "abstinence" or "virginity" pledges. One study in the *Journal of Adolescent Health* found that students who took such pledges were less likely to engage in vaginal sex, but were more likely to engage in oral and anal sex. This may explain why even though teenagers who make pledges have less vaginal intercourse in the short term, they may still have the same level of STIs as their nonpledging colleagues.[12]

For these reasons, many states have rejected abstinence-only education, even if that means having to refuse federal money. By the end of 2008, 24 states had stopped accepting federal funding for abstinence-only education—a major reversal of policy for cash-strapped states caught in an economic downturn. Many of these states based their decisions on the numerous studies that found abstinence-only education was ineffective and that the federal guidelines were too restrictive. As Colorado's chief state medical officer, Dr. Ned Calonge, put it, "To show no benefit compared to nothing. That was striking. . . . These are tax dollars that are going for no useful purpose, and it would not be responsible for us to take those dollars."[13]

Comprehensive sex education provides students with needed information.

If abstinence-only sex education does not work, what does? Many states and educators are returning to comprehensive sex education. As comprehensive sex-education supporter Advocates for Youth defines it:

Comprehensive Sex Education teaches about abstinence as the best method for avoiding STIs and unintended pregnancy, but also teaches about condoms and contraception to reduce the risk of unintended pregnancy and of infection with STIs, including HIV. It also teaches interpersonal and communication skills and helps young people explore their own values, goals, and options.[14]

States Receiving Grants for Abstinence-only Programs

According to the Administration for Children and Families, U.S. Department of Health and Human Services, 28 states received federal grants from federal abstinence education programs in 2008:

- Alabama, $716,369
- Arizona, $776,082
- Arkansas, $440,640
- Florida, $1.9 million
- Georgia, $1.1 million
- Hawaii, $122,091
- Illinois, $1.4 million
- Indiana, $565,556
- Iowa, $238,648
- Kansas, $252,832
- Kentucky, $612,974
- Louisiana, $962,673
- Maryland, $427,257
- Michigan, $1.1 million

- Mississippi, $621,716
- Missouri, $664,196
- Nebraska, $164,055
- Nevada, $210,130
- New Hampshire, $71,177
- North Carolina, $936,723
- North Dakota, $66,744
- Oklahoma, $517,756
- Oregon, $365,772
- South Carolina, $563,972
- South Dakota, $102,285
- Texas, $3.6 million
- Utah, $216,117
- West Virginia, $289,389

Source: Associated Press, "States Receiving Grants," USAToday.com, June 24, 2008. http://www.usatoday.com/news/education/2008-06-24-abstinence-grants_N.htm.

In practice, effective comprehensive sex-education programs have the following characteristics:

- Provide age- and culturally appropriate sexual health information in a safe environment for participants;
- Are developed in cooperation with members of the target community, especially young people;
- Help youths clarify their individual, family, and community values;
- Help youths develop skills in communication, refusal, and negotiation;
- Provide medically accurate information about abstinence and contraception, including condoms;
- Demonstrate clear goals for preventing HIV, other STIs, and/or teen pregnancy;
- Focus on specific health behaviors related to the goals, with clear messages about these behaviors;
- Address psychosocial risk and protective factors with activities to change each targeted risk and to promote each protective factor;
- Respect community values and respond to community needs;
- Rely on participatory teaching methods, implemented by trained educators and using all the activities as designed.[15]

This was the primary method of sex education in public schools from the late 1950s through the 1980s. It was during the 1980s, and then again in the 2000s, that abstinence-only programs gained prominence on the national scene.[16] State politicians, school communities, and parents are returning to comprehensive approaches because of mounting evidence of their effectiveness. In 2007, a study by the nonpartisan National Campaign to Prevent Teen and Unplanned Pregnancy found:

- Abstinence-until-marriage-only programs showed no evidence that they affected teen sexual behavior.
- A large majority of comprehensive sex-education programs provided positive effects on teen sexual behavior, including "delaying the initiation of sex, reducing the frequency of sex, reducing the number of sexual partners and increasing condom or contraceptive use."[17]

The report also debunked several myths propagated about comprehensive sex-education programs. In particular, the study found that comprehensive sex education neither promoted promiscuity nor did it confuse youths. Finally, the report found that these programs had the additional benefit of building confidence and promoted decision-making skills.[18]

An April 2008 study that found teens who took part in comprehensive sex-education programs were less likely to become pregnant than students who had no sex education, and that they had lower teen pregnancy rates than those who participated in abstinence-only programs.[19] It is no wonder that poll after poll shows a vast majority of parents want a broad approach to sex education in schools. While most approved of promoting abstinence, only 15 percent of those polled wanted strict abstinence-only approaches. Most wanted abstinence taught along with information about

> sexually transmitted infections (99%), "how babies are made" (96%), waiting to have intercourse until older (95%), how to make responsible sexual choices based on individual values (91%), how to use and where to get contraceptives (86%), abortion (85%), masturbation (77%), homosexuality (73%), oral sex (72%), and that teens can obtain birth control pills from clinics and doctors without parents' permission (71%).[20]

Above, a teacher conducts a sex-education lesson before her class. What students are taught in such classes depends on a variety of factors. Many schools find themselves being pressured by parents and public officials to provide either "comprehensive" or "abstinence-only" education.

Summary

Providing students with the information they need to be successful in life is what education is all about. Comprehensive sex education has repeatedly provided a better education for students than abstinence-only programs. From lower rates of teen pregnancy to reduced incidence of sexually transmitted infection to more consistent use of condoms and other contraceptives, comprehensive programs outperform all current alternatives. This only makes sense, as comprehensive programs provide students with more information and focus on decision-making skills. These tools equip students to make responsible choices that benefit themselves, their partners, and the community at large. It is time that tax dollars are no longer wasted on programs that do not work and real support is provided for the one approach that consistently performs—comprehensive sex education.

Schools Should Provide Abstinence-Only Education

In 1992, Jason Mesiti and Shannon Silva, 15-year-old students at Chelmsford High School in Springfield, Massachusetts, were required to attend a school assembly. Knowing only that the assembly was an AIDS-awareness program, they were unprepared for what they were about to see. For the next 90 minutes the student body listened to Suzi Landolphi present her *Hot, Sexy and Safer* program. Jason and Shannon quickly realized this was going to be an uncomfortable hour and a half when Landolphi pulled out a condom and had a female student put it over a male classmate's head.[1]

Condoms on the head were only the beginning. Court records allege that during the program, Landolphi

> 1) told the students that they were going to have a "group sexual experience, with audience participation"; 2) used

profane, lewd, and lascivious language to describe body parts and excretory functions; 3) advocated and approved oral sex, masturbation, homosexual sexual activity, and condom use during promiscuous premarital sex; 4) simulated masturbation; 5) characterized the loose pants worn by one minor as "erection wear"; 6) referred to being in "deep sh—" after anal sex; 7) had a male minor lick an oversized condom with her, after which she had a female minor pull it over the male minor's entire head and blow it up; 8) encouraged a male minor to display his "orgasm face" with her for the camera; 9) informed a male minor that he was not having enough orgasms; 10) closely inspected a minor and told him he had a "nice butt"; and 11) made eighteen references to orgasms, six references to male genitals, and eight references to female genitals.[2]

The problems for these students, however, did not end with discomfort during the program. In the weeks that followed, students repeated many of the phrases and reenacted parts of the program during the school day. Mesiti and Silva, along with their parents, brought suit against Landolphi and various members of the school's PTO and district administrators. They alleged that the program violated many of their constitutional rights and created an environment where the students were sexually harassed. The families lost the lawsuit, but the publicity over this program led to an outpouring of interest and support for the litigants, and reignited the debate over sex education in schools.[3]

To the bewilderment of one editorial writer in the *Washington Times*, adults were being allowed to engage in these alleged acts with underage children. Such acts once would get a person thrown in jail. Now they were being used in mandatory school assemblies?[4] This lawsuit and the situation that spawned it highlight one of the perplexing problems with sex education in

America today: What form of sex education is appropriate and effective for students?

What are the options?

Sex education based on delaying sex until marriage has long been a part of the public school model. Beginning in the 1890s, social progressives created educational programs for the schools designed to help students understand their bodies and the role of sex in marriage. The federal government even adopted this approach as it attempted to keep servicemen safe from sexually transmitted infections during both world wars. Then known as "social hygiene," sex education in schools promoted abstinence until marriage and put sex into a pro-marriage and pro-family context. Not surprisingly, this garnered little attention or protest as it fit well with the wishes of parents and communities.[5]

In the 1960s, sex education in the United States took a more controversial approach. With the sexual revolution raging, school programs began providing more information about "safe sex" and included information about such topics as condoms, birth control pills, and abortion. The focus of sex education also shifted. While sex education at the beginning of the century focused on sexual relationships in marriage, sex education in the second half was more concerned with individuals having sex whenever they wanted it, whether married or not. This shift from a committed relationship in marriage to "casual sex" led to numerous problems for society as young people increasingly engaged in high-risk practices.[6]

Schools are now confronted with two choices in providing sex education. The first option is to focus on promoting abstinence—either until marriage (abstinence-until-marriage programs) or at least until students are mature enough and in a committed relationship after the teen years (abstinence-only programs). The other option would be euphemistically labeled "comprehensive" sex-education programs. But "comprehensive" is a misnomer, for while purporting to be a comprehensive approach to sex education, the vast majority of the curriculum is focused on condom use and promotion of questionable activities.[7]

Conversely, abstinence programs focus on keeping teens safe by equipping them with skills they need to avoid sex during their teen years. The federal government has clearly defined abstinence-only programs in legislation that provides funding to states for these programs. In order for a state to qualify for one of these federal block grants, sex-education programs in the state must use curricula that

- Has as its exclusive purpose teaching the social, psychological, and health gains to be realized by abstaining from sexual activity;
- Teaches abstinence from sexual activity outside marriage as the expected standard for all school-age children;
- Teaches that abstinence from sexual activity is the only certain way to avoid out-of-wedlock pregnancy, sexually transmitted diseases, and other associated health problems;
- Teaches that a mutually faithful monogamous relationship in the context of marriage is the expected standard of human sexual activity;
- Teaches that sexual activity outside of the context of marriage is likely to have harmful psychological and physical effects;
- Teaches that bearing children out-of-wedlock is likely to have harmful consequences for the child, the child's parents, and society;
- Teaches young people how to reject sexual advances and how alcohol and drug use increases vulnerability to sexual advances;
- Teaches the importance of attaining self-sufficiency before engaging in sexual activity.[8]

It is important to fight this national problem.

America is facing a crisis. As researchers Christine Kim and Robert Rector wrote in a 2008 Heritage Foundation report, "Each year, some 2.6 million teenagers become sexually active—a rate of 7,000 teens per day. Among high school students, nearly half report having engaged in sexual activity and one-third are currently active."[9] As the study warns, sexually active teenagers are at a greater risk for a variety of dangers, including "sexually transmitted diseases (STDs), reduced psychological and emotional well-being, lower academic achievement, teen pregnancy, and out-of-wedlock childbearing."[10]

The dangers of early sexual activity are well documented. In a 2003 study, the Heritage Foundation found that girls who engaged in sex during their teen years were more likely to contract an STD, have a baby out-of-wedlock, become a single mother, live in poverty, have unstable marriages later in life, and ultimately be less happy.[11] These findings may explain why teens polled by the National Campaign to Prevent Teen Pregnancy have consistently and overwhelmingly stated that they wish they had waited until later before having sex.[12] For some, this remorse over their decision to have sex early has led to severe consequences. In a 2003 study, sexually active teens were more likely to be depressed and had a higher incidence of attempted suicide.[13] Clearly, finding ways of helping teenagers avoid these problems is of national importance.

"Comprehensive" sex education does not work.

In an attempt to control teen pregnancy and stop the spread of sexually transmitted diseases, some educators have promoted sex education under the guise of "comprehensive" sex education instead of abstinence-only approaches. The problem with comprehensive sex education is its failure to be comprehensive. In fact, it fails to address many of the problems confronting teenagers today. Instead of helping teens delay sexual activity, these programs promote sex as long as teens remember to use condoms. Most of these programs are really just the sex-education programs of the 1960s in modern clothing. Surely schools must do better, especially when so much is at stake in the lives of teenagers.[14]

As the lawsuit over the *Hot, Sexy and Safer* presentation at the beginning of this chapter illustrates, communities cannot allow anything and everything into the schools under the guise of sex education. Sadly, Landolphi's presentations are not alone. A 2007 Health and Human Services study examined the most widely used comprehensive sex-education curricula. The findings were most disturbing. Of the nine curricula evaluated, the majority focused almost exclusively on contraception and gave little attention to promoting abstinence. Using a word-count analysis, these programs mentioned condoms 235 times and contraceptives 381 times, while mentioning abstinence only 87 times. This hardly seems "comprehensive."

Instead these programs provided advice on how to get condoms, including, "find stores where you don't have to ask for condoms; wear shades or a disguise so no one will recognize you; have a friend or sibling . . . buy them for you."[15] Other materials involved role playing between the teacher and students, where the teacher would act as the sexual partner and "read more excuses (for not using condoms) and I want you [student] to convince me [teacher] to use a condom."[16]

Finally, many of these curricula focused on sex play involving condoms, including in-class demonstrations where students would practice placing condoms onto penis models or over their fingers. As if the explicitness of these curricula was not enough, the HHS report also found that many contained at least some medically inaccurate or misleading information, all in a curriculum being used with students as young as 13![17]

While the content of these materials is troubling, the most disturbing finding of this study was that these programs have been shown to be of limited effectiveness. While these curricula showed some small improvement in the use of condoms by students, only two demonstrated a positive effect on students delaying sexual activity. One program actually showed that female students were *more* likely to have sex after taking the class than before.[18]

From a public policy standpoint, this is unacceptable. Despite the many problems associated with comprehensive

THE LETTER OF THE LAW

Excerpt from the Sex Education Requirements under the Texas Education Code

Sec. 28.004. LOCAL SCHOOL HEALTH ADVISORY COUNCIL AND HEALTH EDUCATION INSTRUCTION.

(d) The board of trustees shall appoint members to the local school health advisory council. A majority of the members must be persons who are parents of students enrolled in the district and who are not employed by the district. The board of trustees also may appoint one or more persons from each of the following groups or a representative from a group other than a group specified under this subsection:

(1) public school teachers;

(2) public school administrators;

(3) district students;

(4) health care professionals;

(5) the business community;

(6) law enforcement;

(7) senior citizens;

(8) the clergy; and

(9) nonprofit health organizations.

(e) Any course materials and instruction relating to human sexuality, sexually transmitted diseases, or human immunodeficiency virus or acquired immune deficiency syndrome shall be selected by the board of trustees with the advice of the local school health advisory council and must:

(1) present abstinence from sexual activity as the preferred choice of behavior in relationship to all sexual activity for unmarried persons of school age;

sex-education programs, they continue to receive 10 times more government money than abstinence-only programs. This money is being spent on programs that do not even attempt to address the real problem of teen promiscuity and earlier and earlier initiation of sexual activity. Government should stop

(2) devote more attention to abstinence from sexual activity than to any other behavior;

(3) emphasize that abstinence from sexual activity, if used consistently and correctly, is the only method that is 100 percent effective in preventing pregnancy, sexually transmitted diseases, infection with human immunodeficiency virus or acquired immune deficiency syndrome, and the emotional trauma associated with adolescent sexual activity;

(4) direct adolescents to a standard of behavior in which abstinence from sexual activity before marriage is the most effective way to prevent pregnancy, sexually transmitted diseases, and infection with human immunodeficiency virus or acquired immune deficiency syndrome; and

(5) teach contraception and condom use in terms of human use reality rates instead of theoretical laboratory rates, if instruction on contraception and condoms is included in curriculum content.

(f) A school district may not distribute condoms in connection with instruction relating to human sexuality.

(g) A school district that provides human sexuality instruction may separate students according to sex for instructional purposes.

(h) The board of trustees shall determine the specific content of the district's instruction in human sexuality, in accordance with Subsections (e), (f), and (g).

(i) A school district shall notify a parent of each student enrolled in the district of:

(1) the basic content of the district's human sexuality instruction to be provided to the student; and

(2) the parent's right to remove the student from any part of the district's human sexuality instruction.

funding this ineffective approach and instead shift all funding to curricula that promote the values and ideals of families and communities.

Letter from National Abstinence Education Association to President-Elect Barack Obama

November 28, 2008

Dear President-Elect Obama:

As you begin to prioritize the many tasks that lie before you at this historic time, we write on behalf of the millions of students who receive abstinence education. We write as Democrats, as Republicans, as Independents committed to moving beyond the partisan rhetoric that has mischaracterized abstinence education for too long. We also write from our experience working with youth in urban, rural, and suburban neighborhoods. And the stories we hear from them are compelling. They tell us that until abstinence education programs (as currently funded by Congress) came to their school, no one gave them the tools they needed to abstain from sex. Many tell us that even though they had sex in the past, now they are going to wait because of newfound confidence in themselves as a result of abstinence programs. They embody the "yes we can" message enthusiastically!

Millions of youth across the United States are making better health decisions because of the skills they learn in their abstinence education classes. A growing body of research provides compelling evidence that youth who receive abstinence education are significantly less likely to initiate sexual activity as their peers. Sexually experienced students are more likely to discontinue their sexual activity as a result of the skills and encouragement received in abstinence education classes. We cannot turn our backs on this promising evidence just as our youth are responding to the positive message of abstinence as never before.

Research also shows that those students who were a part of an abstinence program, but go on to become sexually active, are no less likely to use a condom than their peers, but still have fewer partners. We know that limiting lifetime partners is important to decreasing the spread of STDs, but avoiding sexual activity is the only way to completely avoid the risk. Beyond the physical consequences,

There is support for abstinence-only sex education.
The federal government has taken notice of the importance of abstinence-only sex education, as evidenced by the financial

however, there are also significant potential emotional consequences to adolescent sexual activity. Abstinence education helps teens avoid these negative, emotional outcomes by empowering them to make decisions that benefit their overall health.

Abstinence is a message that resonates with youth. More and more teens are choosing to abstain but continued support for this initiative is essential given the highly sexualized culture in which they live.

We are writing because like you, we care about the youth of America. We hope you will agree that this must not be a partisan issue. With President Clinton signing Title V abstinence education into law and President Bush signing SPRANS-CBAE abstinence education into law, it is clear that concern for youth crosses both sides of the aisle. It is a public health message that deserves to be continued. As you so aptly stated in your acceptance speech, "we rise or fall as one nation, as one people. Let's resist the temptation to fall back on the same partisanship and pettiness and immaturity that has poisoned our politics for so long." We ask that this be the first campaign promise that you keep. We respectfully ask that you put aside the misinformation you've undoubtedly received about abstinence education and allow for an informed discussion of the facts to determine this important public health policy for our youth. We hope that you will listen and acknowledge the youth who have embraced new opportunities as a result of their abstinence education programs.

We cordially ask that we can meet in order to begin a meaningful and nonpartisan conversation around this issue. We look forward to continuing the important gains that have been made in keeping youth healthy through abstinence education.

Sincerely,
National Abstinence Education Association

Source: http://www.abstinenceassociation.org/docs/action_alerts/Letter_to_President_
Elect_Barrack_Obama.pdf. [sic]

support given to these programs over the years. President Ronald Reagan began the move towards abstinence-only sex education in 1981 when he pushed for $11 million in funding for such programs. Since then, the budget for these programs has increased to the $206 million President George W. Bush sought in 2006. In each of these instances, states requesting the block-grant money from the federal government must demonstrate that they will use the money for abstinence-only programs and will also use matching state money to support these programs.[19]

The reason these programs gain increasing support is because they work. A review of nine studies examining abstinence-based sex education shows that abstinence programs reduce sexual initiation over a twelve month period, reduce the prevalence of casual sex among sexually experienced students, and are effective in reaching inner-city and at-risk students.[20]

The government is not the only one to notice the importance of abstinence education. Studies have shown that parents overwhelmingly support abstinence until marriage and other abstinence-education themes. For instance, a 2003 Zogby poll found that 79 percent of parents supported young people waiting till marriage, or at least waiting till after high school, before engaging in sex. A Heritage Foundation analysis of the polling results led to the conclusion that:

> Only a tiny minority (less than 10 percent) of parents support the values and messages taught in comprehensive sex education curricula. Since the themes of these courses (such as "It's okay for teens to have sex as long as they use condoms") contradict and undermine the basic values parents want their children to be taught, these courses would be unacceptable even if combined with other materials.
>
> The popular culture bombards teens with messages encouraging casual sexual activity at an early age. To counteract this, parents want teens to be taught a

strong abstinence message. Parents overwhelmingly support abstinence curricula that link sexuality to love, intimacy, and commitment and that urge teens to delay sexual activity until maturity and marriage.[21]

Summary

Parents, government agencies, and communities agree that abstinence is a vital goal for teenagers. Early sexual activity leads to a number of problems that will haunt young people for the rest of their lives. In order to combat the pressure to participate in sex early, schools must provide sex education that promotes abstinence. Despite claims to the contrary, "comprehensive" sex-education programs fail to adequately address and promote abstinence in teens. Instead, such programs focus on contraceptives and in some cases even promote sexual activity in teens.

Schools should listen to parents and government leaders and implement abstinence-only sex education in schools. These programs comport with the wishes of parents and provide the positive influences needed for teens to be able to resist the temptation and peer pressure of early sexual activity. Given the consequences, teens deserve nothing less.

The Future of Reproductive Rights

The topic of reproductive rights has long been an area of controversy, and modern technology and current political trends do not indicate a change any time soon. Yet this controversy is not always bad, and in some ways, may push society to deal with conflict through creative problem solving. The future holds both danger and promise, particularly in the areas of new technology, political initiatives, and changes in views about human rights.

Advanced Reproductive Technology

Advances in technology always lead to conflict as society struggles to determine the moral and ethical parameters of the changes technology brings. Nowhere is this more evident than in the field of reproduction. In vitro fertilization was groundbreaking 30 years ago; the first baby conceived outside the womb was labeled "Superbaby" by the media. While the technology now seems commonplace, the controversies surrounding these innovations have hardly died down.[1]

The technologies on the horizon will likely lead to even more ethical struggles. Some scientists predict that 30 years from now it will be possible to take skin cells and transform them into sperm and egg cells, thus allowing for reproduction at any age. Also on the horizon is the ability for parents to know ever more about their baby at the embryonic stage. From an in vitro standpoint, this could mean that parents could choose between the embryos that get implanted based on genetic indicators for tallness, blondness, cancer resistance, etc.[2]

Not everyone is excited about these prospects. Some groups, most notably the Catholic Church, argue that these techniques violate the sanctity of life and could result in doctors playing God.[3] There is also a concern that this is just the beginning of a slippery slope, starting today with in vitro fertilization, and ending in cloning of humans and genetic manipulation in an effort to create "designer babies." These fears are exacerbated by the lack of longitudinal or long-term study of children conceived by in vitro processes. These concerns cause these groups to decry all forms of artificial involvement in reproduction.[4]

New Political Frontiers

The abortion debate has raged since 1973, with neither side having much to show for all of their efforts. Yet the cycle of violence, recrimination, and political jockeying may be giving way to new approaches. For the past several years, factions in both the anti-abortion and abortion-rights movements have come together in an effort to find compromise. In their efforts to see what they have in common, they are able to work toward their shared goals. They hope these efforts will eventually lead to more positive results for all involved. In particular, anti-abortion and abortion-rights groups have sought to jointly address the root problem in the debate. Both sides agree that unwanted pregnancy is the cause for abortions, which ultimately is the center of the debate. If they could find ways to limit or even eradicate unwanted pregnancies, then neither side would need to fight over abortions as they would no longer be needed.[5]

While this new approach to the controversy has certainly not solved the abortion controversy, it is a movement that is gaining

Advanced Reproductive Technology: One Woman's Story

On December 10, 2008, the author interviewed Dr. Brandie Lovelace,[*] a professor at a private, religiously affiliated university in central Texas. Lovelace is the mother of three children, a 9-year-old daughter and 7-year-old fraternal twins. Both of her pregnancies were a result of modern medical advances in reproduction, known as Advanced Reproductive Technology (ARTs). She shared some of her experiences being on the cutting edge of reproductive technology.

"I've wanted children as far back as I can remember," Brandie explained as we sat down to talk about her story. Shortly after getting married, she and her husband began trying to start the family they had always wanted, with no success. After trying to get pregnant for almost a year, Brandie visited a reproductive endocrinologist—a doctor that specializes in fertility issues.

Brandie and her husband were tested in a number or ways. For her husband, this meant one test to check his sperm and make sure they were correctly shaped and moving fast enough. She had far more tests. "For women, there are many tests they can do to check on fertility issues. They all hurt. For men, only one, rather painless, test." After several rounds of being poked, prodded, and injected, the doctor explained that she had endometriosis—tissue problems in the uterus—and this was making it hard for her to get pregnant.

She was put on a round of shots designed to promote egg production and required to keep careful record of her fertility cycle. The chemicals she took gave her hot flashes, cramps, and mood swings. When one treatment would not work, she would be shifted to another. Although these changes in treatment took their toll on her physically and emotionally, she persevered because, as she said, "no matter how much it hurt, at least I knew I was trying." After more than a year of procedures, she became pregnant.

ground. Nowhere is this more evident than in radio ads that ran in several states during the campaign. The language of the ad was clear and simple:

> With 1 in 5 pregnancies in America ending in abortion and the number of abortions unchanged from 32 years

For her first pregnancy, the process known as "artificial insemination" was used. When the time came, Brandie's husband produced a sperm sample that was then injected directly into her uterus. The procedure took, and 38 weeks later, the Lovelaces had a healthy baby girl.

One year later, the Lovelaces decided to try again. Because they had moved, they had to find a new fertility doctor. Their new doctor explained that he did not do artificial insemination because the risks were too great for multiple children and there was too little control of the process. Instead, he suggested they try the more aggressive in vitro fertilization. This procedure involved giving Brandie high doses of hormones and other chemicals so that her body would produce a large number of egg cells all at the same time. After they reached a certain stage, these eggs would be harvested and then doctors would insert individual sperm cells into eggs outside the womb. After being fertilized, a number of these eggs were then put back into Brandie's uterus for the rest of the pregnancy. This procedure was uncomfortable, and definitely more expensive, but had a good success rate.

Succeed it did. The fertilized eggs that were placed in her womb successfully attached; she became pregnant with twins.

It had taken her seven years to get pregnant. During the ensuing years, she endured daily shots, frequent pain, almost $20,000 in out-of-pocket expense (insurance covered some parts of the process), and extensive strains on her marriage. The results were three beautiful children.

So in the end, was it worth it?

"Some people will go to the ends of the Earth, others aren't willing to take the first step. For me, I would sacrifice anything for my babies." Brandie said, smiling. "I would definitely do it all again."

*The names of all involved have been changed to protect the medical privacy of the participants.

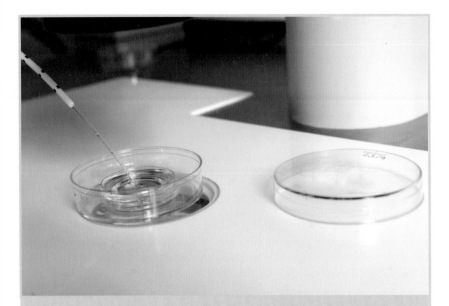

An embryo is created in a Petri dish in a laboratory. Advancements in technology will likely lead to additional ethical issues pertaining to reproductive rights. Should parents be allowed to select embryos with certain genetic traits? Should genetic manipulation of embryos or human cloning be legalized? And what should be done with embryos created in laboratories that will not be implanted in their mothers' wombs?

ago, it's time to stop the political posturing and get serious about protecting life.

2,400 late-term abortions a year is tragic, but what often gets ignored is that 10 times more infants die each year in America largely because of inadequate healthcare. We need to ask ourselves what it really means to be pro-life and help move the conversation beyond bumper sticker slogans.

Thankfully, some lawmakers are already working on real solutions that will drastically reduce abortions by expanding programs that encourage adoption, increasing pre- and post-natal healthcare, preventing unintended pregnancies, and helping young mothers choose life.

It's time for Democrats and Republicans to come together around solutions based on results, not rhetoric.[6]

The most controversial, and to many unexpected, part of this ad is that it was sponsored by the anti-abortion group Faith in Public Life. While some expect continued shouting past one another, this group and others like it on both sides of the debate have begun to look for deeper solutions.[7]

During the debates of the 2008 presidential campaign, Barack Obama mentioned common-ground approaches as a way of dealing with the abortions controversy. The method of looking for core common interests may also be useful in other areas of controversy, from sex education in public schools to protecting the rights of women and children.[8]

New Legal Frontiers

Reproductive rights are also moving arenas, as jurisprudence involving birth control, abortion, education, and other relevant matters is shifting out of the federal courts and into state courts. Some legal scholars theorize that reproductive rights will be worked out at the state level, with courts looking to state constitutions and state laws. Some have long argued that the abortion debate began in the states and should have been allowed to work its way out there. Even if it did not start there, however, it seems the future is now in the state courts and legislatures.[9]

Human-rights groups are advocates of the newest areas of reproductive rights. Those active in human rights around the world have attempted to change the way reproductive rights are spoken of and thought about. Those on the forefront of the movement to protect reproductive rights have begun to argue that describing this issue as a matter of "rights" does a disservice to women. This argument is based on the idea that rights language is not enough because rights are protected when a person uses the legal system to force the issue. Many women do not have

Do Men Have Reproductive Rights?

Discussions of reproductive rights often focus on the rights of the woman to control her reproductive life and capabilities. An area that receives little attention involves the rights of the man. A woman has a right to an abortion, but what rights do men have when it comes to reproduction? Does a man have a right to terminate a pregnancy? Does a man have any recourse if a pregnancy is achieved through fraud?

This issue came into sharp relief in 2005 in the case of *Phillips v. Irons*. In the complaints filed, Dr. Richard Phillips claimed that he should not be responsible for the child of his former lover, Dr. Sharon Irons. Phillips claimed that Irons saved his sperm after engaging in oral sex and used it to impregnate herself in an attempt to get him to leave his wife. The courts ultimately found that Irons had the rights to Phillips' sperm, as it was a freely given gift. Therefore she could do with it as she pleased.*

The results of this case left more questions than answers. Groups have sprouted up around the country to try to shift attention onto the rights of men and examine whether there are fairness issues that need to be addressed. For now, however, one author put it best:

Men's rights must be balanced with the rights of society as a whole and, at this time, the best balance is achieved by promoting the interests of the child over those of the parents. Men must take all precautions necessary to avoid facing the liability of an unanticipated child being brought into their lives, just as women should. In order to avoid this problem completely, men should be able to fully trust their sexual partners before engaging in any sexual activity and should take their own preventative measures, such as providing their own contraception. Until there is a radical change in the conception process as we know it, men's reproductive rights will continue to be suppressed in order to provide for the greater good.**

Phillips v. Irons, 2005 WL 4694579, (Ill. Appeals Court) (2005).

**Drake Law Review* 1013, 1056 (Summer 2007).

the resources to hire attorneys and otherwise pursue such action in courts. Therefore, advocates argue that all these issues should be couched in terms of reproductive health, and some go so far as to argue that it should be described as the duty or responsibilities of society in protecting reproductive health, instead of rights that the individual has to pursue on their own.[10]

Summary

From the hopeful new couple seeking to expand their family to the abortion protester standing outside a clinic on a cold winter day, the questions of reproductive rights offer a broad array of issues, conflicts, and conscience-rending decisions. The tone of the conflict may change, and the technology involved will inevitably change. Yet despite the different approaches and worldviews that participants have, the fact that both sides of these debates believe that they are doing what is best for other people is heartening. As long as people are still doing their best at doing what is right, then maybe there is hope at the end of the conflict after all.

Beginning Legal Research

The goals of each book in the Point-Counterpoint series are not only to give the reader a basic introduction to a controversial issue affecting society, but also to encourage the reader to explore the issue more fully. This Appendix is meant to serve as a guide to the reader in researching the current state of the law as well as exploring some of the public policy arguments as to why existing laws should be changed or new laws are needed.

Although some sources of law can be found primarily in law libraries, legal research has become much faster and more accessible with the advent of the Internet. This Appendix discusses some of the best starting points for free access to laws and court decisions, but surfing the Web will uncover endless additional sources of information. Before you can research the law, however, you must have a basic understanding of the American legal system.

The most important source of law in the United States is the Constitution. Originally enacted in 1787, the Constitution outlines the structure of our federal government, as well as setting limits on the types of laws that the federal government and state governments can enact. Through the centuries, a number of amendments have added to or changed the Constitution, most notably the first 10 amendments, which collectively are known as the "Bill of Rights" and which guarantee important civil liberties.

Reading the plain text of the Constitution provides little information. For example, the Constitution prohibits "unreasonable searches and seizures" by the police. To understand concepts in the Constitution, it is necessary to look to the decisions of the U.S. Supreme Court, which has the ultimate authority in interpreting the meaning of the Constitution. For example, the U.S. Supreme Court's 2001 decision in Kyllo v. United States held that scanning the outside of a person's house using a heat sensor to determine whether the person is growing marijuana is an unreasonable search—if it is done without first getting a search warrant from a judge. Each state also has its own constitution and a supreme court that is the ultimate authority on its meaning.

Also important are the written laws, or "statutes," passed by the U.S. Congress and the individual state legislatures. As with constitutional provisions, the U.S. Supreme Court and the state supreme courts are the ultimate authorities in interpreting the meaning of federal and state laws, respectively. However, the U.S. Supreme Court might find that a state law violates the U.S. Constitution, and a state supreme court might find that a state law violates either the state or U.S. Constitution.

Not every controversy reaches either the U.S. Supreme Court or the state supreme courts, however. Therefore, the decisions of other courts are also important. Trial courts hear evidence from both sides and make a decision, while appeals courts review the decisions made by trial courts. Sometimes rulings from appeals courts are appealed further to the U.S. Supreme Court or the state supreme courts.

Lawyers and courts refer to statutes and court decisions through a formal system of citations. Use of these citations reveals which court made the decision or which legislature passed the statute, and allows one to quickly locate the statute or court case online or in a law library. For example, the Supreme Court case Brown v. Board of Education has the legal citation 347 U.S. 483 (1954). At a law library, this 1954 decision can be found on page 483 of volume 347 of the U.S. Reports, which are the official collection of the Supreme Court's decisions. On the following page, you will find samples of all the major kinds of legal citation.

Finding sources of legal information on the Internet is relatively simple thanks to "portal" sites such as findlaw.com and lexisone.com, which allow the user to access a variety of constitutions, statutes, court opinions, law review articles, news articles, and other useful sources of information. For example, findlaw.com offers access to all Supreme Court decisions since 1893. Other useful sources of information include gpo.gov, which contains a complete copy of the U.S. Code, and thomas.loc.gov, which offers access to bills pending before Congress, as well as recently passed laws. Of course, the Internet changes every second of every day, so it is best to do some independent searching.

Of course, many people still do their research at law libraries, some of which are open to the public. For example, some state governments and universities offer the public access to their law collections. Law librarians can be of great assistance, as even experienced attorneys need help with legal research from time to time.

Common Citation Forms

Source of Law	Sample Citation	Notes
U.S. Supreme Court	*Employment Division v. Smith*, 485 U.S. 660 (1988)	The U.S. Reports is the official record of Supreme Court decisions. There is also an unofficial Supreme Court ("S. Ct.") reporter.
U.S. Court of Appeals	*United States v. Lambert*, 695 F.2d 536 (11th Cir.1983)	Appellate cases appear in the Federal Reporter, designated by "F." The 11th Circuit has jurisdiction in Alabama, Florida, and Georgia.
U.S. District Court	*Carillon Importers, Ltd. v. Frank Pesce Group, Inc.*, 913 F.Supp. 1559 (S.D.Fla.1996)	Federal trial-level decisions are reported in the Federal Supplement ("F. Supp."). Some states have multiple federal districts; this case originated in the Southern District of Florida.
U.S. Code	Thomas Jefferson Commemoration Commission Act, 36 U.S.C., §149 (2002)	Sometimes the popular names of legislation—names with which the public may be familiar—are included with the U.S. Code citation.
State Supreme Court	*Sterling v. Cupp*, 290 Ore. 611, 614, 625 P.2d 123, 126 (1981)	The Oregon Supreme Court decision is reported in both the state's reporter and the Pacific regional reporter.
State Statute	Pennsylvania Abortion Control Act of 1982, 18 Pa. Cons. Stat. 3203-3220 (1990)	States use many different citation formats for their statutes.

Cases

Roe v. Wade, 410 U.S. 113 (1973)
The Supreme Court determined that a woman has a right to an abortion during the first trimester of the pregnancy, but that the state has an interest in regulating abortion after the first trimester, and a compelling interest in the pregnancy once the fetus becomes viable.

Planned Parenthood v. Danforth 428 U.S. 52 (1976)
The Court found that states cannot outlaw certain methods of abortion nor can they require a married woman to get her husband's consent before an abortion, but they can require minors to get parental consent as long as judicial bypass options are available.

Maher v. Doe, 432 U.S. 526 (1977)
The Court delcared there was no right to state funding for abortions, even if indigent women are covered for other pregnancy items.

Bellotti v. Baird, 443 U.S. 622 (1979)
The Court overturned parental notice and consent laws where no judicial bypass is available.

Harris v. McRae, 448 U.S. 297 (1980)
The Court upheld Hyde Amendment that restricts federal funding for abortions.

Akron v. Akron Center for Reproductive Health, 462 U.S. 416 (1983)
The Court struck down laws restricting abortion in the first trimester.

Webster v. Reproductive Health Services, 492 U.S. 490 (1989)
The Court found state facilities are not required to perform abortions.

Ohio v. Akron Center for Reproductive Health, 497 U.S. 502 (1990); *Hodgson v. Minnesota,* 497 U.S. 417 (1990)
Parental notification was found to be constitutional as long as there is a judicial bypass option.

Rust v. Sullivan, 500 U.S. 173 (1991)
The Court upheld a ban on federal funding for abortion counseling.

Planned Parenthood v. Casey, 505 U.S. 833 (1992)
The Court upheld *Roe,* but rejected the trimester model, focusing instead on viability.

Schenk v. Pro-Choice Network, 519 U.S. 357 (1997)
The Court upheld fixed buffer zones, but struck down "floating" buffer zones as an unconstitutional infringement on free speech.

Stenberg v. Carhart, 530 U.S. 914 (2006)
The Court overturned Nebraska's ban on "partial-birth" abortions.

Ayotte v. Planned Parenthood of Northern New England, 546 U.S. 320 (2006)
The Supreme Court found that notification and wait laws must include a provision for medical emergency or are unconstitutional.

Gonzales v. Carhart and Gonzales v. Planned Parenthood Federation of America, **127 S. Ct. 1610 (2007)**
The Court upheld federal ban on partial-birth abortions.

Terms and Concepts

abortion
abstinence
abstinence-only sex education
birth control
claims of conscience
comprehensive sex education
condoms
contraceptives
penumbras
right to privacy

Introduction: Reproductive Rights

1 Linda Gordon, *The Moral Property of Women: A History of Birth Control Politics in America.* Chicago: University of Illinois Press, 2002, p. 8.
2 Dr. Larry S. Milner. "History" Society for the Prevention of Infanticide (1998). http://www.infanticide.org/history.htm.
3 Milner, Society for the Prevention of Infanticide. Also Emma Dickens, *Immaculate Contraception.* London: Robson Books, 2000.
4 Gordon, *Moral Property of Women*, pp. 14–16.
5 Ibid.
6 Genesis 38: 3–10.
7 Dickens, *Immaculate Contraception*, pp. 17–18. Gordon, *Moral Property of Women*, pp. 19–20.
8 Dickens, *Immaculate Contraception*, pp. 60–62. Gordon, *Moral Property of Women*, pp. 19–21.
9 Dickens, *Immaculate Contraception*, p. 18. Linda Gordon, *Woman's Body, Woman's Right: Birth Control in America.* New York: Penguin Books, 1990, pp. 29–32.
10 Gordon, *Woman's Body, Woman's Right*, p. 32.
11 Gordon, *Moral Property of Women*, pp. 7–10.
12 Gordon, *Woman's Body, Woman's Right*, pp. 49–60.
13 Ibid., p. 57.
14 American Experience. "The Pill." PBS. org. http://www.pbs.org/wgbh/amex/pill/peopleevents/e_comstock.html.
15 Daniel DeNoon. Birth Control Timeline. WebMD, July 17, 2003. http://www.medicinenet.com/script/main/art.asp?articlekey=52188.
16 Center for Disease Control. "Margaret Sanger." http://www.cdc.gov/mmwr/preview/mmwrhtml/mm4847bx.htm; Also, Dickens, pp. 86–96.
17 Ibid.
18 *New York v. Sanger*, 222 N.Y. 192 (1918).
19 *United States v. One Package*, 13 F. Supp. 334 (1936).
20 *Griswold v. Connecticut*, 381 U.S. 479 (1965). *Eisenstadt v. Baird*, 405 U.S. 438 (1972).
21 *Planned Parenthood of Central Missouri, et al. v. Danforth*, 428 U.S. 52 (1976).
22 *Maher v. Roe*, 432 U.S. 464 (1977). *Harris v. McRae*, 448 U.S. 297 (1980).
23 *Planned Parenthood of Southeastern Pennsylvania v. Casey*, 505 U.S. 833 (1992), 901.
24 Id.; and *Gonzales v. Carhart*, 550 U.S. 124, 2007.
25 E.J. Dionne Jr., "Litmus Test for Hypocrisy," *Washington Post.* Feb. 13, 2007: p. A21.
26 David L. Hudson Jr., "Abortion Protests & Buffer Zones." Firstamendmentcenter. org, January 26, 2007. http://www.firstamendmentcenter.org//assembly/topic.aspx?topic=buffer_zones&SearchString=abortion_buffer_zone).
27 DeNoon, *Birth Control Timeline.*
28 DeNoon, *Birth Control Timeline.*
29 U.S. Department of Health and Human Services, Center for Disease Prevention, "Maternal Mortality and Related Concepts," *Vital and Health Statistics* 3, no. 33 (February 2007): p. 7.
30 Jeffrey P. Brosco, "The Early History of the Infant Mortality Rate in America: A Reflection Upon the Past and a Prophecy of the Future," *Pediatrics.* 103, no. 2 (February 1999): pp. 478–485.

Point: Access to Contraceptives Should Be Liberalized

1 Sondra Goldschein, "Religious Refusals and Reproductive Rights: Accessing Birth Control at the Pharmacy," ACLU Reproductive Freedom Project. New York: American Civil Liberties Union, 2007, p. i.
2 Ibid., p. 3.
3 Association of Reproductive Health Professionals, "Health Benefits of Contraception," *Brochures for Patients.* 1996. http://www.arhp.org/Publications-and-Resources/Patient-Resources/printed-materials/hbc.
4 *Carey v. Population Services International*, 431 U.S. 678 (1977): p. 695.
5 Rachel K. Jones and Heather Boonstra, "Confidential Reproductive Health Services for Minors: The Potential Impact of Mandated Parental Involvement for Contraception," *Perspectives on Sexual and Reproductive Health.* 36, no. 5 (September/October

2004). http://www.guttmacher.org/pubs/
psrh/full/3618204.pdf.

6 *Lundman v. McKown,* 530 N. W. 2d.
807 (1995). Also Jennifer Stanfield,
"Current Public Law and Policy Issues:
Faith Healing and Religious Treatment
Exemptions to Child-Endangerment
Laws: Should Parents be Allowed to
Refuse Necessary Medical Treatment for
their Children Based on Their Religious
Beliefs?" 22 *Hamline Journal of Public
Law & Policy.* 45 (Fall 2000).

7 *Ohio v. Akron Center for Reproductive
Health,* 497 U.S. 502 (1990), and *Hodgson v. Minnesota,* 497 U.S. 417 (1990).

8 Sexuality Information and Education
Council of the United States.
"Women Sue Wal-Mart Over Access
to Emergency Contraception."
http://www.siecus.org/index.
cfm?fuseaction=Feature.showFeature&f
eatureid=1339&pageid=483&parentid=
478.

9 Ibid.

10 Associated Press. "Wal-Mart to Stock
Emergency Contraception Pill,"
USAToday.com, March, 3, 2006.
http://www.usatoday.com/money/
industries/retail/2006-03-03-walmart-
contraception-pills_x.htm.

11 Goldschein, "Religious Refusals and
Reproductive Rights," p. 4.

12 Ibid.

13 Loren Stein. "Covering Birth Control:
Why One Woman Sued." WebMD,
September 4, 2000. http://www.
medicinenet.com/script/main/
art.asp?articlekey=51391. Also,
American Pregnancy Association.
"Health Insurance for Pregnant
Women." October 2008. http://
www.americanpregnancy.
org/planningandpreparing/
affordablehealthcare.html.

14 Stein, "Covering Birth Control."

**Counterpoint: Contraceptives
Should Be Closely Monitored and
Regulated**

1 *Neil Noesen v. Medical Staffing,* U.S. 7th
Cir. Court of Appeals, No. 06-2831, May
2, 2007.

2 Ibid. Also, Associated Press. "Judge
Dismisses Wal-Mart Pharmacist's

Contraception Suit." Foxnews.com,
June 2, 2006. http://www.foxnews.com/
story/0,2933,198030,00.html.

3 Joy Victory. "Pharmacists Suspended
After Refusing to Dispense 'Morning
After Pill.'" ABCNews.com, December
12, 2005. http://abcnews.go.com/Health/
story?id=1391310.

4 Tracy C. Shuman, ed. "Birth Control
Pills: Your Guide." WebMD.com,
February 1, 2006. http://www.webmd.
com/sex/birth-control/birth-control-
pill?page=3.

5 Holly Mead, "Making Birth Control
More Accessible to Women: A Cost Benefit Analysis of Over-The-Counter Oral
Contraceptives," Institute for Women's
Policy Research, Briefing Paper. Feb.
2001. http://www.iwpr.org/pdf/otc0201.
pdf.

6 Brett Andrew Johnson, "Insertion and Removal of Intrauterine
Devices," *American Family Physician.*
January 1, 2005. http://www.aafp.org/
afp/20050101/95.html.

7 Planned Parenthood. "Diaphragm."
May, 15, 2008. http://www.
plannedparenthood.org/health-topics/
birth-control/diaphragm-4244.htm.

8 *Carey v. Population Services International,* 431 U.S. 678 (1977).

9 *Meyer v. Nebraska,* 262 U.S. 390 (1923).

10 *Pierce v. Society of Sisters,* 268 U.S. 510
(1925).

11 *Prince v. Commonwealth of Massachusetts,* 321 U.S. 158 (1944).

12 *Wisconsin v. Yoder,* 406 U.S. 205 (1972).

13 Ibid.

14 Charles Babington, "McCain Dodges
Question on Vigra, Birth Control,"
Houston Chronicle. July 10, 2008.
http://www.chron.com/disp/story.mpl/
front/5880162.html.

15 Geraldine Sealey. "Erections Get Insurance; Why Not the Pill? Women See
Progress in Getting the Birth Control
Pill Covered." ABCNews.com. June
19, 2002. http://abcnews.com/US/
story?id=91538.

16 Caroline Bollinger, "Access Denied,"
Prevention. September 22, 2004. http://
www.prevention.com/cda/article/access-
denied/a9a466263d803110VgnVCM200

00012281eac____/health/healthy.living.
centers/ob.gyn.health.
17 Ibid.

Point: Abortion Should Not Be Restricted by Government or Others

1 Douglas Kmiec, "The Day I Was Denied Communion for Endorsing Obama," excerpted from *Can a Catholic Support Him?*. Beliefnet.com, September 16, 2008. http://blog.beliefnet.com/stevenwaldman/2008/09/the-day-i-was-denied-communion.html.

2 Ibid.

3 Ibid.

4 Associated Press. "Priest: No communion for Obama voters." MSNBC.com. November, 13, 2008. http://www.msnbc.msn.com/id/27705755/.

5 Barack Obama, *The Audacity of Hope*. New York: Crown, 2006, pp. 197–198.

6 *Gonzales v. Carhart*, (Ginsburg dissent), 550 U.S. 124 (2007).

7 Ibid, at sec. I.A.

8 BBC. "Women's Rights Arguments in Favor of Abortion: Abortion and Bodily Rights," BBC.com. http://www.bbc.co.uk/ethics/abortion/mother/for_3.shtml.

9 Jeb Rubenfeld, "On the Legal Status of the Proposition that 'Life Begins at Conception,'" 43 *Stanford Law Review* 43, no. 599 (1991): pp. 609–610.

10 Nancy J. Hirschmann, "Abortion, Self-Defense and Involuntary Servitude," 13 *Texas Journal of Women & Law*. 41 (2003): p. 49.

11 *See generally*, James Risen and Judy L. Thomas, *Wrath of Angels*, New York: Basic Books, 1998.

12 *See generally*, Patricia Baird-Windle and Eleanor J. Bader, *Targets of Hatred: Anti-Abortion Terrorism*. New York: Palgrave, 2001.

13 Rickie Solinger, ed., *Abortion Wars: A Half Century of Struggle, 1950–2000*. Berkeley: University of California Press, 1998, p. xi.

14 National Abortion Federation. "Safety of Abortions." http://www.prochoice.org/pubs_research/publications/downloads/about_abortion/safety_of_abortion.pdf.

15 Linda Gordon, *The Moral Property of Women: A History of Birth Control Politics in America*. Chicago: University of Illinois Press, 2002, p. 299.

16 Nancy Felipe Russo and Henry P. David, "When Pregnancies are Unwanted," *Psychology & Reproductive Choice*, March, 5, 2002. http://www.prochoiceforum.org.uk/psy_ocr2.asp.

17 *Wrath of Angels*, pp. 373–377.

18 Ibid. Also, *Schenk v. Pro Choice Network of Western New York*, 519 U.S. 357 (1997).

19 *Schenck v. United States*, 249 U.S. 47 (1919).

20 *Schenk v. Pro Choice Network*.

21 Guttmacher Institute, "An Overview of State Abortion Laws," January 1, 2009.

22 Janessa L. Bernstein, "The Underground Railroad to Reproductive Freedom: Restrictive Abortion Laws and the Resulting Backlash," *Brooklyn Law Review*. 73, Rev. 1463 (2008): pp. 1477–1480.

23 *Gonzalez v. Carhart*, 550 U.S. 124 (2007).

24 N.E.H. Hull and Peter Charles Hoffer, *Roe v. Wade: The Abortion Rights Controversy in American History*. Lawrence: University Press of Kansas, 2001, p. 279.

Counterpoint: Abortion Should Be Heavily Regulated and Eventually Outlawed

1 U.S. Department of Health and Human Services. "HHS Secretary Calls on Certification Groups to Protect Conscience Rights." March 14, 2008. http://www.hhs.gov/news/press/2008pres/03/20080314a.html.

2 U.S. Department of Health and Human Services. "Health and Human Services Issues Final Regulation to Protect Health Care Workers From Discrimination." December 18, 2008. http://www.hhs.gov/news/press/2008pres/12/20081218a.html.

3 Joe Messerli. "Should Abortion Be Banned." BalancedPolitics.org, October 20, 2008. http://www.balancedpolitics.org/abortion.htm.

4 Konstantinos Kapparis, *Abortion in the Ancient World*. London: Gerlad Duckworth, 2002: pp. 39–40.

5 Ibid., pp. 174–194.

6 Norman Ford, *When Did I Begin*. Cambridge University Press, Cambridge: 1991, pp. 57–75.

7 Robert F. Cochran Jr., "Evangelicals, Law, and Abortion," *Faith and Law: How Religious Traditions from Calvinism to Islam view American Law*. Robert F. Cochran Jr., ed. New York: New York University Press, 2008.

8 Donna Lee Bowen, "Abortion, Islam and the 1994 Cairo Population Conference," *International Journal of Middle East Studies*. Vol. 29, num 2 (1997): pp. 161–184.

9 _____. "What Orthodox Jews Believe." Beliefnet.com. January 2008. http://www.beliefnet.com/Faiths/2001/06/What-Orthodox-Jews-Believe.aspx.

10 William James Larson, *Human Embryology and Teratology*. New York: Churchill Livingston, 1998, cited in Rich Deem. "Science and Abortion: The Scientific Basis for a Pro-Life Position." Godandscience.org. July 23, 2007. http://www.godandscience.org/doctrine/scienceabortion.html.

11 National Right to Life Committee. "President Bush Signs Unborn Victim of Violence Act into Law, After Dramatic One-vote Win in Senate." April 6, 2004. http://www.nrlc.org/Unborn_victims/BushsignsUVVA.html.

12 National Right to Life Committee. "State Homicide Laws that Recognize Unborn Victims." June 25, 2008. http://www.nrlc.org/Unborn_victims/Statehomicidelaws092302.html.

13 *Roe v. Wade*, 410 U.S. 113 (1973): pp. 163–164.

14 *Planned Parenthood v. Casey*, 505 US 833 (1992): p. 833.

15 Ibid., p. 847.

16 Ibid., p. 873.

17 Ibid., p. 877.

18 Ibid., p. 885.

19 *Casey* (1992) pp. 900–901.

20 Ibid., pp. 901–902.

21 Ibid., pp. 888–889.

22 Guttmacher Institute, "An Overview of State Abortion Laws," January 1, 2009.

23 Ibid.

24 Tom Curry. "Roberts, Alito Help Define New Supreme Court." MSNBC.com. June 18, 2007. http://www.msnbc.msn.com/id/19244921/.

Point: Schools Should Provide Students with Comprehensive Sex Education

1 "About the Film," *Point of View: The Education of Shelby Knox*, POV series, Public Broadcasting System. http://www.pbs.org/pov/pov2005/shelbyknox/about.html.

2 Janet E. Rosenbaum, "Patient Teenagers? A Comparison of the Sexual Behavior of Virginity Pledgers v. Matched Non-Pledgers," *Pediatrics*. 123, no. 1 (January 2009): pp. e110–e120.

3 Rob Stein, "Premarital Abstinence Pledges Ineffective, Study Finds," *Washington Post*, December 29, 2008.

4 Rebekah Saul, "Whatever Happened to the Adolescent Family Life Act?" *Guttmacher Report on Public Policy*. 1, no. 2 (April 1998). http://www.guttmacher.org/pubs/tgr/01/2/gr010205.html.

5 Joshua H. Silavent, "Abstinence Only Education: Is It Really Effective?" *Atlanta Life* (September 2008): p. 9. http://www.abstinenceassociation.org/docs/Point-Counterpoint_Sept_08.pdf.

6 House Committee on Government Reform—Minority Staff, Special Investigation Division, "The Content of Federally Funded Abstinence-Only Education Programs." Report prepared for Henry Waxman, December 2004. http://oversight.house.gov/documents/20041201102153-50247.pdf.

7 Ibid.

8 Jacqueline E. Darroch, et al., "Differences in Teenage Pregnancy Rates Among Five Developed Countries: The Roles of Sexual Activity and Contraceptive Use," *Family Planning Perspectives*. 33, no. 6 (November/December 2001). http://www.guttmacher.org/pubs/journals/3324401.html.

9 Elizabeth Landau, "Report: Teen Pregnancies Up for the First Time in 15 Years." CNN.com. July 11, 2008. http://www.cnn.com/2008/HEALTH/07/10/teen.pregnancy/index.html.

10 U.S. Centers for Disease Control and Prevention, "Nationally Representative CDC Study Finds 1 in 4 Teenage Girls Has a Sexually Transmitted Disease." http://www.

cdc.gov/STDConference/2008/media/
release-11march2008.htm. Christopher
Trenholm, et al., "Impact of Four Title
V, Section 510 Abstinence Education
Programs (Final Report)," *Mathematica
Policy Research*, 2005.

11 J. Santelli, et al., "Abstinence-only education policies and programs: A position
paper of the Society for Adolescent
Medicine," *Journal of Adolescent Health*.
38 (2006): pp. 83–87.

12 Brückner and Bearman, "After the Promise," pp. 271–278.

13 Associated Press, "States Turn Down
Abstinence Education Grants."
USAToday.com. June 24, 2008.
http://www.usatoday.com/news/
education/2008-06-24-abstinence-
grants_N.htm.

14 Advocates for Youth, "Sex Education
Programs: Definitions and Point
by Point Comparisons," May 2008.
http://www.advocatesforyouth.org/rrr/
definitions.htm.

15 Brigid McKeon. "Sex Education:
Programs and Curricula," Advocates
for Youth, 2006. http://www.
advocatesforyouth.org/publications/
factsheet/fssexcur.htm.

16 See generally, Kristen Luker, *When Sex
Goes To School: Warring Views on Sex—
and Sex Education—Since the Sixties*.
New York: W.W. Norton, 2006.

17 Jeorg Dreweke. "Review of Key
Findings of 'Emerging Answers 2007'
Report on Sex Education Programs."
Guttmacher Institute, November 2007.
http://www.guttmacher.org/media/
evidencecheck/2007/11/07/Advisory_
Emerging_Answers_2007.pdf.

18 Ibid.

19 Pamela K. Kohler, et al., "Abstinence-
Only and Comprehensive Sex Education
and the Initiation of Sexual Activity and
Teen Pregnancy," *Journal of Adolescent
Health*. 42, no. 4 (April 2008): pp. 344–
351.

20 Santelli, et al., "Abstinence and Abstinence-only Education," pp. 72–81.

Counterpoint: Schools Should Provide Abstinence-Only Education

1 *Brown v. Hot, Sexy and Safer*, 68 F.3d
525, 528–530 (1995).

2 Ibid., p. 530.

3 Bob Holer, "State AIDS educator
criticizes Chelmsford program", *Boston
Globe*. August 27, 1993.

4 "Sex Education or Sexual Harassment?"
Washington Times, March 13, 1994.

5 Kristen Luker, *When Sex Goes To School*,
pp. 44–62.

6 Ibid.

7 National Abstinence Education Association. "Straight From the Source: What
so called 'Comprehensive' Sex Education
Teaches to America's Youth." June 2007.
http://www.abstinenceassociation.org/
docs/NAEA-Straight_from_the_Source.
pdf.

8 U.S. Social Security Act, Sec. 510(b)(2).
http://www.ssa.gov/OP_Home/ssact/
title05/0510.htm.

9 Christine Kim and Robert Rector,
"Abstinence Education: Assessing the
Evidence," Heritage Foundation, *Back-
grounder*. 2126 (April 27, 2008): p. 1.

10 Ibid.

11 Robert Rector, et al. "The Harmful
Effects of Early Sexual Activity and
Multiple Sexual Partners Among
Women: A Book of Charts." Heritage
Foundation, June 23, 2003: pp. 5–6. http://
www.heritage.org/Research/Family/
upload/44695_2.pdf.

12 Bill Albert. "With One Voice 2007:
America's Adults and Teens Sound
Off About Teen Pregnancy." National
Campaign to Prevent Teen Pregnancy,
February 2007: p. 26. http://www.
thenationalcampaign.org/resources/pdf/
pubs/WOV2007_fulltext.pdf.

13 Robert Rector, et al. "Sexually Active
Teenagers Are More Likely to Be
Depressed and to Attempt Suicide."
Center For Data Analysis Report 03–04,
Heritage Foundation, June 3, 2003.
http://www.heritage.org/Research/
Abstinence/cda0304.cfm.

14 Patra Stephan. "HHS Report:
'Comprehensive' Sex Education
Ineffective and Offensive." National
Association for Abstinence
Education, June 13, 2007. http://www.
abstinenceassociation.org/newsroom/
pr_061307_hhs_report_comprehensive.
html.

15 Administration for Children and Families. "Review of Comprehensive Sex Education Curricula." Department of Health and Human Services, May 2007: p. 6. http://www.acf.hhs.gov/programs/fysb/content/abstinence/06122007-153424.PDF.

16 Ibid.

17 Ibid., p. 7.

18 Ibid., p. 8.

19 Facts & Stats from "The Education of Shelby Knox." PBS.org. http://www.pbs.org/pov/pov2005/shelbyknox/special_overview.html.

20 National Abstinence Education Association. "Abstinence Works! Studies Validating the Efficacy of Abstinence Education." April 12, 2007. http://www.abstinenceassociation.org/docs/NAEA_Abstinence_Works_041207.pdf.

21 Robert Rector, et al., "What Do Parents Want Taught in Sex Education Programs?" Heritage Foundation, *Backgrounder.* 1722 (January 28, 2004). http://www.heritage.org/Research/Abstinence/bg1722.cfm.

Conclusion: The Future of Reproductive Rights

1 Helen Pearson, "Making Babies: The Next 30 Years," *Nature.* 454 (July 16, 2008): pp. 260–262.

2 Ibid.

3 Cathy Lynn Grossman. "Catholic Church Updates Code on Birth Technology." USAToday.com, Dec. 12, 2008. http://www.usatoday.com/news/religion/2008-12-12-biomed-catholic_N.htm.

4. Pearson, "Making Babies," p. 261.

5 Search for Common Ground. "The Common Ground Network for Life and Choice." SFCG.org. http://www.sfcg.org/Programmes/us/us_life.html.

6 Steve Waldman. "Shocking Radio Ad Pushes for Common Ground Abortion Reduction." Beliefnet.com, October 29, 2008. http://blog.beliefnet.com/stevenwaldman/2008/10/unusual-radio-ads-push-for-com.html.

7 Ibid.

8 _____. "Obama Should Seek Common Ground on Abortion Debate with Ryan-DeLauro Bill." *Medical News Today,* January 7, 2009. http://www.medicalnewstoday.com/articles/134595.php.

9 Scott A. Ross and Douglas M. Raines, "The Intriguing Federalist Future of Reproductive Rights," 88 *Boston University Law Review* 175. (2008).

10 Helen Irving, *Gender and the Constitution: Equity and Agency in Comparative Constitutional Design.* New York: Cambridge University Press, 2008, pp. 196–198.

Books

Baird-Windle, Patricia, and Eleanor J. Bader. *Targets of Hatred: Anti-Abortion Terrorism.* New York: Palgrave, 2001.

Bennett, Belinda ed. *Abortion (The International Library of Medicine, Ethics and Law).* Burlington, Vt.: Ashgate Publishing, 2004.

Cochran Jr., Robert F., ed. *Faith and Law: How Religious Traditions from Calvinism to Islam View American Law.* New York: New York University Press, 2008.

Cook, Rebecca J., Bernard M. Dickens, and Mahmoud F. Fathalla. *Reproductive Health and Human Rights: Integrating Medicine, Ethics, and Law.* Oxford: Clarendon Press, 2003.

Dickens, Emma. *Immaculate Contraception.* London: Robson Books, 2000.

Farber, Daniel A. *Retained by the People: The "Silent" Ninth Amendment and the Constitutional Rights Americans Don't Know They Have.* New York: Basic Books, 2007.

Feldman, David M. *Marital Relations, Birth Control, and Abortion in Jewish Law.* New York: Schocken Books, 1974.

Goodman, Richard A., editor-in-chief. *Law in Public Health Practice,* 2nd ed. New York: Oxford University Press, 2007.

Gordon, Linda. *The Moral Property of Women.* Chicago: University of Illinois Press, 2002.

Hull, N.E.H. and Peter Charles Hoffer. *Roe v. Wade: The Abortion Rights Controversy in American History.* Lawrence: University Press of Kansas, 2001.

Irvine, Janice M. *Talk About Sex: The Battles Over Sex Education in the United States.* Berkeley: University of California Press, 2002.

Konstantinos, Kapparis. *Abortion in the Ancient World.* London: Duckworth, 2002.

Luker, Kristin. *When Sex Goes to School: Warring Views on Sex—and Sex Education—Since the Sixties.* New York: W.W. Norton, 2006.

Mundy, Liza. *Everything Conceivable: How Assisted Reproduction is Changing Men, Women, and the World.* New York: Alfred A. Knopf, 2007.

Obama, Barack. *The Audacity of Hope.* New York: Crown, 2006.

Risen, James, and Judy L. Thomas. *Wrath of Angels.* New York: Basic Books, 1998.

Solinger, Rickie, ed. *Abortion Wars: A Half Century of Struggle, 1950–2000.* Berkeley: University of California Press, 1998.

Web Sites

Center for Reproductive Rights
http://www.reproductiverights.org
The CRR's Web site provides reports and other information about reproductive rights.

Guttmacher Institute
http://www.guttmacher.org
Through an interrelated program of social science research, public education and policy analysis, the Guttmacher Institute provides numerous reports and studies about a variety of areas related to reproductive rights.

The Heritage Foundation
http://www.heritage.org
This conservative research institute has created a number of studies involving sex education and adolescent sexual activity.

MedicineNet.com
http://www.medicinenet.com
An online health care media publishing company, MedicineNet is a good source for general medical information that is balanced and easy to understand.

National Abstinence Education Association
http://www.abstinenceassociation.org
NAEA provides links to reports and information about the benefits of abstinence education.

National Organization for Women
http://www.now.org
NOW's Web site provides information on abortion rights, access to birth control, and sex education information.

National Right to Life
http://www.nrlc.org
The NRLC, a lobbying and activist organization, offers materials on the prevention of abortions.

Planned Parenthood
http://www.plannedparenthood.org
The Planned Parenthood Web site is a good source of information on a range of issues related to reproductive rights.

PICTURE CREDITS

JOHN E. FERGUSON JR. is on faculty at Baylor University in Waco, Texas, where he teaches Negotiation and American Constitutional Development. He is a Baptist minister as well as an attorney who is licensed in Tennessee, Washington, D.C., and with the Supreme Court of the United States. Receiving both his law and divinity degrees from Vanderbilt University, Ferguson has worked in 34 states providing mediation and conflict resolution training based on constitutional principles. He has authored numerous books and scholarly articles. Ferguson lives with his wife, Merideth, and their two sons outside of Waco.

ALAN MARZILLI, M.A., J.D., lives in Birmingham, Ala., and is a program associate with Advocates for Human Potential, Inc., a research and consulting firm based in Sudbury, Mass., and Albany, N.Y. He primarily works on developing training and educational materials for agencies of the federal government on topics such as housing, mental health policy, employment, and transportation. He has spoken on mental health issues in thirty states, the District of Columbia, and Puerto Rico; his work has included training mental health administrators, nonprofit management and staff, and people with mental illnesses and their families on a wide variety of topics, including effective advocacy, community-based mental health services, and housing. He has written several handbooks and training curricula that are used nationally—as far away as the territory of Guam. He managed statewide and national mental health advocacy programs and worked for several public interest lobbying organizations while studying law at Georgetown University. He has written more than a dozen books, including numerous titles in the POINT/COUNTERPOINT series.